Transfer of Farm Technology and Communication Skills

NIPA GENX ELECTRONIC RESOURCES & SOLUTIONS P. LTD.
New Delhi-110 034

Transfer of Farm Technology and Communication Skill

C. Satapathy

(Retd.), Professor and Dean
Department of Extension
Odisha University of Agriculture and Technology
Bhubaneswar-751003, Odisha

M.P. Nayak

Joint Director of Extension (Information)
Odisha University of Agriculture and Technology
Bhubaneswar-751003, Odisha

NIPA GENX ELECTRONIC RESOURCES & SOLUTIONS P. LTD.
New Delhi-110 034

NIPA GENX ELECTRONIC RESOURCES & SOLUTIONS P. LTD.

101,103, Vikas Surya Plaza, CU Block
L.S.C.Market, Pitam Pura, New Delhi-110 034
Ph : +91 11 27341616, 27341717, 27341718
E-mail:newindiapublishingagency@gmail.com
www: www.nipabooks.com

For customer assistance, please contact
Phone: + 91-11-27 34 17 17 Fax: + 91-11- 27 34 16 16
E-Mail: feedbacks@nipabooks.com

ISBN: 978-93-91383-99-2

Composed and Designed by NIPA.

Acknowledgement

We greatly acknowledge the sources known as unknown to write the book. We have used references to make the book as per requirement. The authors are duly acknowldged sources used in writing the book.

Authors

Preface

Transfer of farm Technology is a complex process involving social sciences, scientists, farmers and extension experts. To transfer farm technology each and every actor in the process needs to be familiar with communication skill.

In Extension Education greater emphasis is given in teaching, research and field extension work. The authors out of their lifelong experiences have realized the need for effective communication. The present book is written out of such realization. The book is designed for use by extension scholars, scientists and field professionals. The book may help to be good communicators for farmers residing in rural areas.

Authors

Contents

1

Transfer of Farm Technology

1.1 Agricultural technologies and knowledge

Agricultural technologies and knowledge have, until recently, largely been created and disseminated by public institutions. But over the past two decades, biotechnology for agricultural production has developed rapidly, and the world economy has become more globalised and liberalised. This has boosted private investment in agricultural research and technology, exposing agriculture in developing countries to international markets and the influence of multinational corporations. But the public sector still has a role to play, particularly in managing the new knowledge, supporting research to fill any remaining gaps, promoting and regulating private companies, and ensuring their effects on the environment are adequately assessed.

A new way to approach technology transfer

The new economic and scientific context requires a new, more complex, model for transferring technology. The evolving model has four main components: knowledge management, gap filling research, promotion and regulation of the private sector, and environmental impact analysis (see Figure 1).

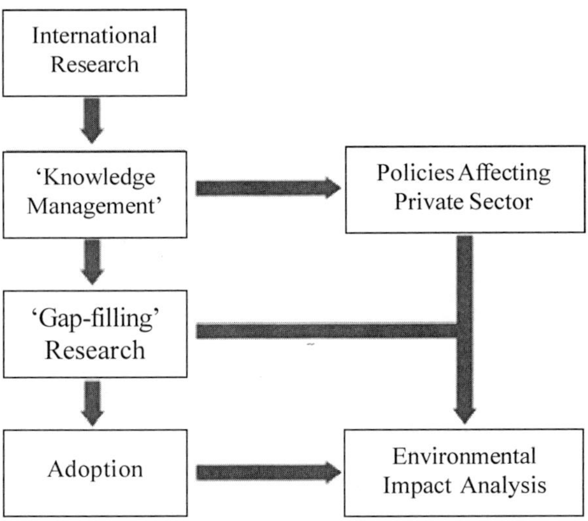

Figure 1. A multidimensional model of agricultural technology transfer for the public sector

Knowledge management

The public sector continues to be largely responsible for knowledge management -that is, articulating national needs, matching them to scientific opportunities, mobilising available technology, and adjusting them to farmers' needs.

NARIs and universities undertake this role in many developing countries. They help develop both new and crops, promote successful agriculture in poor ecological conditions and tackle small-scale technological problems, none of which greatly interest the private sector. Such work accounts for much of the research done by local institutions, and needs to be strengthened. Local institutions should provide incentives for their staff to collaborate with international researchers and seek synergies with research done elsewhere. In many ways the CGIAR centres are important in helping integrate local efforts with the knowledge available worldwide.

Gap-filling research

National public research institutions also have a major responsibility for research in areas ignored by the private sector. This 'gap filling research' is particularly relevant to technologies that are not embodied in physical products-for example, forage management, animal health, and soil management and conservation and irrigation practices.

Public research into agriculture in developing countries represents about a quarter of worldwide expenditure in agricultural research. But it needs to be managed effectively if it is to produce high quality research to complement internationally available technologies and help developing countries acquire and use them. Some countries, like Brazil, China, India and Vietnam, have already taken action, using careful planning and working with research institutions in developed countries' research institutions to help focus research.

Promoting and regulating the private sector

The public sector should also both promote private investment and regulate private companies. Several policies can help encourage the private sector to invest in technologies that are relevant to farmers in developing countries.

First, adequate intellectual property rights legislation can be put in place. This allows private companies to protect profits from their research, helping attract investors and promoting research.

Second, tax and credit facilities can provide indirect economic incentives to investment.

Third, setting up frameworks for turning new technologies, like seeds or agrochemicals, into commercial realities-for example consistent bio-safety regulations, royalty agreements, profit sharing and reinvestment-can be used to encourage interactions between private firms and public institutions, supporting joint activities and, thereby, encouraging technology transfer.

Environmental impact analyses

Meanwhile, policymakers must be considering the environmental consequences of agricultural research. New agricultural technologies often use natural resources intensively, potentially damaging the environment, for example through land degradation or water contamination. This is especially true if the new technology is imported without being tested in local conditions. Genetically modified crops are a good example. Developing countries like Argentina largely rely on industrialised nations to provide genetically modified breeds. Close to 90 per cent of Argentina's soybean crop is transgenic, and this has proved highly profitable in the past ten years. But the full environmental effects of expanding to marginal areas, displacing other crops and livestock, and using crop rotations are still unknown.

Policymakers can help by developing regulatory measures, like mandatory environmental impact assessments, to minimise potential environmental damage and to protect consumers.

1.2 Transfer of farm technology

India has developed vast agricultural research system. The system encompasses teaching, research and extension system. The major thrust has been transfer of research to the farmer's field through extension system. The three systems are interdependent. The transfer of technology is thus comes within domain of Extension system. To understand the complexities in technology transfer system there is need to have operational definition of the term 'transfer of technology'.

1.2.1 Concept and definitions of technology transfer

There is number of definitions and concepts as how to describe transfer of technology. Some of them are cited here for better insight into the content of the terms used,

i) Transfer of technology is the process of bringing out well tested and usable farm technologies from research stations to the field of the users.

ii) Transfer of technology not only indicate the transfer of technology to the users but also acceptance as use as per recommendation.

iii) The transfer of technology is the adoption of the technology by the users to the extent of their satisfaction.

iv) Transfer of technology denotes dissemination and translation of technology into action

v) Transfer of technology is the process by which well tested and location specific technologies are transferred through appropriate channels of communication to the users and enter into farming system providing expected benefits to the users.

vi) Transfer of technology may be defined as dissemination of technical know-how to the hands of the users irrespective of sources for higher outputs.

vii) Transfer of technology is that part of Extension Education which covers communication, adoption, diffusion and program decision to make farming communities better than existing situation.

1.2.2 Dimensions of transfer of technology

Transfer of technology is not limited to certain specific variables. It is complex and multi disciplinary approach. The concept is wide and far reaching. It is so because transfer of technology encompasses man, material and money. The extension experts call three important ingredients in transfer of technology as (i) Technology generation (ii) Technology Transfer and (iii) Technology use.

I. Technology Generation system.

The technology generation is the process by which the new ideas, practices and innovations are produced. The system required well qualified scientists, resources and infrastructures to produce desirable technologies. The technologies produced face the problems of adoption and non-adoption. In case of non-adoption the technologies are refined or modified to fit into requirement of the users. The system is also known as feedback and feed forward. The adoptable technologies are to be judged on the following parameters for wider acceptance and use.

Desirable quality of farm technology

1. Based on needs of the client
2. Relatively more advantageous
3. Simple to adopt
4. Compatible to farming system
5. Location and farmer specific
6. Relatively more profitable than existing one
7. In the line of Govt. Policy
8. Tuned with knowledge, skill and attitude of the users
9. Market demand
10. Sustainability

II. Technology Transfer system

Technology transfer system is relatively difficult than technology generation. This system operates with motivation, persuasion which lead to favourable decision by the users

Factors associated with Technology Transfer system

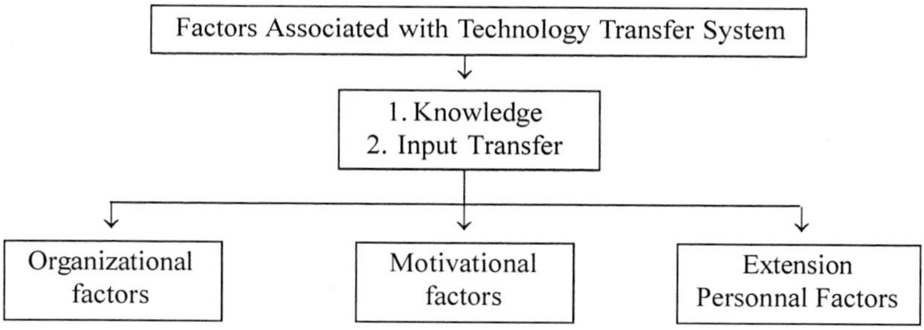

1. Organizational factors

Formal extension program operates through well defined organization. The transfer of technology depends on efficiency of the organization. The followings are parameters to judge structural and functional aspects that promote transfer of technology.

i) Structure of department

ii) Well defined extension program

iii) Supervision

iv) Market linkage

v) Research linkage

vi) Monitoring mechanism

vii) Evaluation approach from human point of view

2. Motivational factor

The most important and complex dimension in transfer of technology is motivational factor. The adoption of technology after transfer is possible only on favourable decision of the technology users. To motivate farmers for adoption of technology is linked with amount of information is beamed into farmer's community. The important channels of farm technology are:

i) Personal contact

ii) Group approach

iii) Mass media

iv) Demonstration
v) Farm literature
vi) Field day
vii) Farmer's exposure to research station
viii) Other means of motivation

3. Extension personnel factors

Transfer of technology is very much related to back ground of extension personnel who are in charge of the extension program at block level. The following factors help in acceleration of transfer of technology:

i) Competency
ii) Back ground
iii) Training of extension personnel
iv) Sincerity and commitment
v) Attitude towards farming and farmer
vi) Problem solving aptitude
vii) Challenging nature
viii) Technical knowledge

III. Technology user system

The users of technology are special segment in the process of technology transfer. They take the final decision to accept and use the technology. This system is influenced by different factors like personal, socio- cultural, economic and environmental.

Factors of Technology System

Personal Variables	Socio-Cultural Variables	Economic Variables	Environmental Variables
1. Age	1. Caste	1. Land size	1. Soil
2. Educate	2. Religion	2. Annual income	2. Temperature
3. Decision taking ability	3. Social participation	3. Annual investment	3. RainFALL
4. Orietation	4. Leadership ability	4. Labour force	4. Cropping pattern
5. Cosmopoliteness	5. Social system	5. Family size	5. Input availability
6. Change proneness	6. Value system	6. Farm power	6. Credit
7. Innoativeness	7. Economic rationality	7. Irrigation facility	7. Extension contact
8. Entrepreunership orientation	8. Commercal	8. Occupation	8. Marketing facility
		9. Market link	9. Govt. policy

The communication skill dealt in this book aims at informing the scientists of the Krishi Vigyan Kendra (KVK). At present KVKs are the important formal extension organization for transfer of technology in addition to State Development Departments like Agriculture, Horticulture, Animal husbandry, Fisheries forestry and Home science. The scientists of KVK need to know the communication skill required to transfer technology to the farming communities.

All KVKs fall under the jurisdiction of one of the 11 Agricultural Technology Application Research Institutes (ATARIs) throughout India. As of May 2021, there were approximately 722 KVKs throughout India.

PHILOSOPHY OF KVK

The philosophy of KVK is to accelerate production in agriculture and allied fields through application of science and technology. It impart s training through work experience i.e. learning by doing and to improve the socioeconomic conditions of the weaker section of the society by generating self employment opportunities.

Krushi Vigyan Kendras are the district level farm science centres established by Indian Council of Agricultural Research (ICAR for speedy transfer of technology to farmer's field. The KVK s aim at increasing productivity on a sustainable basis and creating opportunities for greater economic activities in agriculture and allied sector. The KVKs identify technological needs of the farming community and endeavour to meet the needs through activities like technology assessment and refinement, organization of training program, demonstration, and exhibition, Field days, campaign, publication of technical literature in local language.

Concept of KVK

The KVKs identify the technological needs of the area, constraints in growth of agriculture and develop strategies for removal of these bottlenecks.

1. To accelerate production of agriculture and allied fields through application of science and technologies.
2. To impart training through work experience, i.e. learning by doing.
3. To improve socio economic condition of he weaker section of the society by generating self employment opportunities.

Objectives of KVK

1. Planning and conducting survey of the area to identify gap in adoption of technology and training needs of the area.

2. Undertaking on-arm testing to assess and refine technology as per local condition
3. Planning and conducting production oriented .need based short and duration training courses both on-campus and off-campus
4. Organize farm far science club in villages and rural schools
5. Developing and maintaining demonstration units on scientific lines for training and demonstration purpose
6. Imparting training to field level extension personnel of the state, bank and non-government agencies.
7. Conducting first line demonstrations for adoption of improved production technology
8. Providing farm advisory service to the farmers.

The mandate of KVK

The mandates of KVK is Technology Assessment and Demonstration for its Application and Capacity Development.

- On-farm testing to assess the location specificity of agricultural technologies under various farming systems.
- Frontline demonstrations to establish production potential of technologies on the farmers' fields.

The first KVK was established in 1974 at Pondicherry. The KVK scheme is 100% financed by Govt. of India and the KVKs are sanctioned to Agricultural Universities, ICAR institutes, related Government Departments and Non Government Organizations (NGOs) working in Agriculture.

Present status of KVK in India

S.No.	State	Number of KVK by Now
1	Himachal Pradesh	13
2	Jammu & Kashmir	18
3	Ladhakh (UT)	04
4	Punjab	22
5	Uttarakhand	13
6	Delhi	01
7	Haryana	18
8	Rajasthan	44
9	Uttar Pradesh	86
10	Bihar	44

11	Jharkhand	24
12	A & N Islands	03
13	Odisha	33
14	West Bengal	23
15	Assam	26
16	Arunachal Pradesh	17
17	Sikkim	04
18	Manipur	09
19	Meghalaya	07
20	Mizoram	08
21	Nagaland	11
22	Tripura	08
23	Maharastra	49
24	Gujarat	30
25	Goa	02
26	Chattisgarh	28
27	Madhya Pradesh	54
28	Tamil Nadu	32
29	Puducherry	03
30	Andhra Pradesh	24
31	Telengana	16
32	Karnataka	33
33	Kerala	14
34	Lakshadweep	01
	Total	**722**

2

Communication: A Tool for Transfer of Technology

2.1 Communication comes from word

'Communi' means common. To establish commonness between two individuals is communication. Communication is to share information, idea, and attitude or tuned together for a particular message. We may say that any action done is communication. On an average, about 70% of the active hours per day is spent by an individual on communication. It comes about 10-12 hours per day an individual spends to communicate his ideas, meaning, intention or to receive them.

The communication is much more important when we are assigned of responsibility to communicate technologies to the receivers.

2.2 Nature of communication

Many authors have narrated nature of communication and advantages in different manner keeping the need and importance of the area they deal. These are mostly,

1. Leads to personal effectiveness
2. Help to establish network with people
3. Helps to collaborate with others while in work place
4. Helps in motivation to perform better.
5. Leads to better understanding between and among people
6. Creates better interpersonal relation
7. Increases listening capacity
8. Creates better environment to face resistance if any.

2.3 Definitions of communication

Review of literatures reveals that authors have defined communication in various ways. Some impotent definitions are presented to provide insight to the concept of communication:

Author		
1.	Brooker (1949)	Communication is anything that conveys meaning that carries a message from one person to another
2.	Schramme 1954	When we communicate, we are trying to establish commonness with someone, i.e., we are trying to share information an idea or attitude. In essence it is an act of getting a sender and receiver tuned together for a particular message or a series of messages.
3.	Dickey&Zelco 1955	Communication is the process of inducing others to interpret an event, fact, opinion or situation in accordance with the intent of the speaker
4.	Steinberg 1958	The act of communicating in a public relation sense involves the relying or transmitting of signal or symbol verbals, written, or pictorial symbol from a specific source to a specific audience or recover by means of any one of the several media that act as channel for transmission of the symbol
5.	Roger and Yost 1960	Communication is the flow of research finding a from Agriculture scientist to the farmer
6.	Stevens 1960	Communication is the discriminating response of an organism to a stimulus
7.	Paul Leagan 1961	Communication is the process by which two or more people exchange ideas, facts, feelings, or impression in ways that each gains a common understanding of meaning intent and use of message
8.	Newmen & Summer 1962	Communication is the process of exchanging facts ideas opinions emotions by two or more persons. The exchange is successful only when mutual understanding result. Merely saying is not communication. Receiver and sender may or may not agree but communication has occurred when one at least understands what other means to convey
9.	Hovland 1964	Communication may be defined as process by which an individual the communicator transmits (usually verbal) to modify behaviour of other individuals
10.	Weaver 1964	Communication is all of procedures by which our mind can affect

The definitions use some specific words like transactional process, multi level process, cultural interaction, disseminating process, transformal process, and dynamic process psychological process to explain what communication is.

All these definitions lead to conclude simply that Communication is expression of an idea which may be verbal, non-verbal or vocal that is perceived, heard or read by another person.

2.4 The intent and content of communication

We communicate our ideas to receiver. What we have in mind or our thought should perfectly be expressed to get feedback. The thought and expression is intent and content of communication. Any communication is bound to be positive and pleasant when we are positive to communicate and receive message. Positive communication is minus of negative thoughts and words are closely connected with the communicator's existing frame of mind and the core competencies. Our concern is that sender of the message should have ability to translate his thought perfectly or express correctly so the receiver gets a clear message to give feedback.

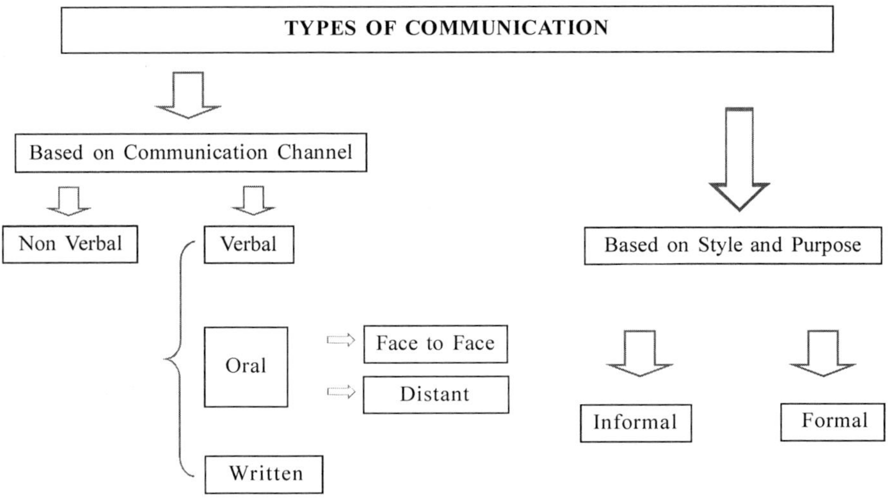

2.5 Types of communication

Different types of communication are,

Types of Communication

1. Non-Verbal communication

Nonverbal communication refers to gestures, facial expressions, tone of voice, eye contact (or lack thereof), body language, posture, and other ways people can communicate without using language.

2. Verbal communication

Verbal communication is the use of sounds and words to express you, especially in contrast to using gestures or mannerisms (non-verbal communication). An example of verbal communication is saying "No" when someone asks you to do something you don't want to do

i) Oral communication

Oral communication is the process of verbally smiting information and ideas from one individual or group to another. Oral communication can be either formal or informal. Examples of informal oral communication include:

a) **Face-to-face Communication:** Few examples of face-to-face communication include general conversation, meetings, sales pitches, interviews and the illusive night out with a date.

b) **Distant communication:** Executives can receive urgent text messages during a meeting, in the car or at the airport and relay important decisions immediately. Email is an excellent tool for business and personal communication. Scheduling can be accomplished via text messages or email

ii) Written communication

Well-written communication helps define goals, identify problems and arrive at solutions. This is important in every aspect of business. Executives must clearly write memos so that staff understands the directives without confusion.

3. Informal communication

Informal Communication is the casual and unofficial form of communication wherein the information is exchanged spontaneously between two or more persons without conforming the prescribed official rules, processes, system, formalities and chain of command.

4. Formal communication

Formal communication refers to interchange of information officially. The flow of communication is controlled and is a deliberate effort. This makes it possible for the information to reach the desired place without any hindrance, at a little cost and in a proper way.

1. **Interpersonal communication** is the process of exchange of information, ideas, feelings and meaning between two or more people through verbal and/or non-verbal methods. It often includes face-to-face exchange of messages, which may take form of a certain tone of voice, facial expressions, body language and gestures.

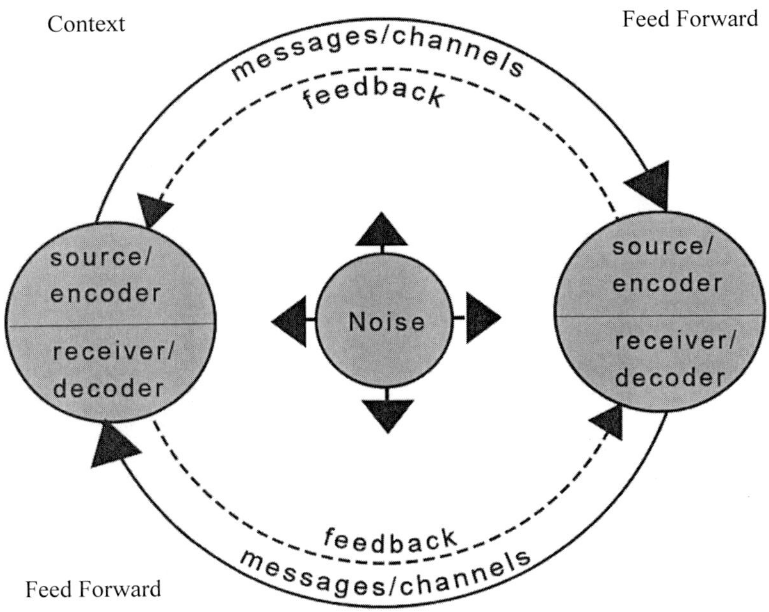

Fig. The Process of interpersonal Communication

Types of communication we frequently meet with

1. Interpersonal communication
2. Organizational communication
3. Mass communication
4. Social communication
5. Transformational communication.
6. Corporate communication
7. Group communication

1. Interpersonal communication

In case of interpersonal communication individual communicates through his mind following thinking and feeling. By doing so he processes the information he wants to transmit. In this case interaction between and more persons takes place. This communication provides scope to express core feeling of an individual. The degree of exchange of owns feeling and idea is much higher than other forms of communication.

2. Organizational communication

Things such as performance feedback, training, delegation, policy statements, directions or orders are all examples of downward communication. Horizontal communication occurs between organizational members who are on the same level in the managerial hierarchy of the organization. Without a positive communication climate no organization can either function or survive the complexities that besiege it every day. Communication takes place constantly in an organization.

3. Mass communication

Mass communication is the process of imparting and exchanging information through mass media to large segments of the population. It is usually understood for relating to various forms of media, as these technologies are used for the dissemination of information, of which journalism and advertising are part.

4. Social communication

Social communication is the use of language in social contexts. It encompasses social interaction, social cognition, pragmatics, and language processing.

5. Transformational communication

Transformational communication is about transferring meaning, not information. Transformational communication happens through establishing an emotional connection. The recipient needs to feel something. Without feeling, without a genuine connection, we end up with just the illusion that communication has taken place.

6. Corporate communication

Corporate communication is the practice of developing, cultivating and maintaining a corporate identity or brand image. A solid corporate communications team provides initiatives to mold company image, communicate with internal and external audiences, and sustain a long-term positive reputation.

7. Group communication

The term "group communication" refers to the messages that are exchanged by group members. The messages that are exchanged by group members provide evidence of the nature of the group. The messages that are exchanged identify whether the group is a social group or a task group.

2.6. The process of communication

The process of communication means that message goes from sender to the receiver through which media with what results. There are certain ingredients in communication process which are put to action. The basic ingredients are source or sender, message, channel, receiver and feedback. These ingredients are responsible to have communication process. Many authors have cited these ingredients of communication with addition or deletion of some other ingredients.

Elements of communication

Author	Ingredients
1. Aristotle	1. Speaker 2. Speech 3. Audience
2. Shanon-Weaver	1. Source 2. Transmitter 3. Signal 4. Receiver 5. Destination
3. Paul Leagan	1. Communicator 2. Message 3. Channel 4. Audience
4. S-M-C-R model	1. Source 2. Message 3. Channel 4. Receiver
5. Harlod, Lasswell, Claude, Shannon, Weaver	1. Source 2. Transmitter 3. Signal 4. Receiver 5. Destination
6. Emery	1. Source 2. Channel 3. Message 4. Receiver 5. Feedback
7. Berlo	1. Communication source 2. Encoder 3. Message 4. Channel 5. Decoder 6. Communication Reviver

Summarising the different models of communication process and elements involved therein, the communication process can be better understood by the following elements.

1. The sender
2. The sender has an idea
3. The sender encodes idea into message
4. The message travels through a channel
5. Noise in the transmission process
6. The receiver receives the message
7. The receiver decodes the message
8. The receiver provides he feedback
9. The frame of reference of the sender and receiver
10. The context of the receiver

2.6.1. The Sender/Source/Communicator

The sender of the message can be any individual from whom the message is originated. The credibility of the source is very important determinant in the success of communication. To evoke correct response he should give right touch to the message.

COMMUNICATOR/SOURCE/SENDER

1. Initiates purposeful message
2. Directs message to audience to produce effect
3. Carries faith in message to inform audience
4. Communicates to audience to create friendly situation to make them understood
5. Communicator keeps himself well informed to communicate message

A good communicator with credibility can communicate very well. Very good and popular speakers earn credibility. The audience of receiver of the message judge the credibility of the source to receive message and act upon.

A number of studies have clearly shown the impact of credibility of the source on effectiveness of communication.

Components of the credibility are

Communicatoe/Source/Sender

Should know Interested in	**Should be skill in**	**Should have**	**Should prepare**
1. His objective	1. Welafe of audience	1. Selection of message	1. Plan of communication
2. His audience communication	2. Result of his materials and equipment	2. Treatment of message	2. Communication
3. His message channel l	3. Communication in oral and written	3. Expressing message	3. Plan for evaluation
4. His organizing ability	4. Process of communication	4. Selection and use of message	4. Format for collection of feedback
5. His professional ability		5. Understanding of audience	
		6. Evaluation of impact	

2.6.2 Message

The physical production of the source is the message for the receiver. It may be speech, writing, picture or movement of body we want the receiver should receive, understand accept and act upon.

Message is the information a communicator wishes his audience to receive comfortably. Messages are composed of symbols having a meaning. Encoding means translation of idea by the source to be transferred as message. The information, idea, attitude, appeal, argument, feeling, or anything to offer to receiver is the content of message.

There are three important aspects of message

Message code: A code can be defined as any group of symbols that can be structured in ways that is meaningful to some persons. The language is code through which we express our ideas

Message content: The contents are the materials in the message that are selected by source to express his purpose

Message Treatment: The decision which the source makes in selecting and arranging both code and content

When we prepare message for consumption of the audience specially farmers in agriculture there is need to ensure the following desirable qualities of the message to get good result.

Desirable qualities of message

1. Convincing	10. Manageable
2. Pertinent to need of the receiver	11. Complete
3. In the line of the objectives to achieve	12. Concise
4. Clear understanding	13. Simple
5. As per social and economic needs.	14. Newness in nature
6. Accurate	15. Attractive to catch attention
7. Timely	16. Practicable
8. Based on research finding	17. Rewarding
9. Applicable to field condition	18. Immediate problem solving

2.6.3 Channel of communication

A communication channel is the medium, mean, manner or method through which a message is sent to its intended receiver. The basic channels are written (hard copy print or digital formats), oral, spoken, electronic and multimedia.

Channel is the means by which a message travels from source to receiver. It is the path through which message is physically transmitted.

We refer public media as channel like TV, radio, film etc. These are called mass media. The interpersonal channel is those involve face to face exchange between source and receiver 'words'

Selection of channel for transfer of message. There are certain factors that determine the selection of channel. These are,

1. What channels are available
2. Preference of source to use channel
3. Impact of channel
4. Cost effectiveness
5. Adaptable to the content of the message
6. Knowledge level of the receiver.

Obstruction in Channel

Many obstructions may enter into channel creating disturbances in receiving the message. We call it NOISE.

1. Failure of channel: In meeting all cannot receive message equally. The channels create problem. The audience have frequent complain about this.
2. Failure on the part of the communicator to handle channel skilfully.
3. Failure to select appropriate channel suiting to the message
4. Failure to use channel as per ability of the receivers
5. Failure on the part of receiver to listen or look at the channel

Classification of NOISE

1. Physical noise: Noise from outside
2. Physiological impairment, deaf, handicap
3. Choice of words to convey the meaning
4. Syntactical problem: Structure of sentence and grammatical problem
5. Psychological problem. When mind of the receiver is not ready to receive message
6. Social noise. When message is not compatible with social value and norm.

2.6.4 Feedback

In the communication process, feedback refers to a response from the receiver

That gives the communicator an idea of how the message is being received and whether it needs to be modified.

Feedback in communication means action and reaction of the receiver to the message. It helps the sender to understand message is received and understood.

Types of feedback

There are four types of constructive feedback:

1. Negative feedback – corrective comments about past behaviour.
2. Positive feedback – affirming comments about past behaviour.
3. Negative feed forward – corrective comments about future performance.
4. Positive feed forward – affirming comments about future behaviour.

2.6.5 Receiver of the message

The receiver is an individual like sender. When he responds to the message he becomes the sender. Therefore both are same but only role changes. Therefore there is no need to deal about receiver separately. In short the process of communication involves the following steps.

1. The sender
2. The sender has an idea
3. The sender encodes the idea into a message
4. The message travels through the channel
5. Noise in the transmission process
6. The receiver gets the message

7. The receiver decodes the massage
8. The receiver provides the feedback
9. The frame of reference of the sender and receiver
10. The context of the receiver

1. The sender

The sender of the message can be any individual The individual wishes to communicate anything is the sender of the message.

2. The sender has an idea

The idea is called stimuli. The sender may have a basket of good ideas but all ideas cannot be processed at one time. He has to give priority to process which idea first. The back ground of the sender enables him to predict correctly as which idea the receiver will accept. All the senders feel that their ideas are good and will be accepted by the receivers. This is not true. The ideas of the sender face resistance by the receiver. The success of communication depends on the ability of the sender to predict accurately how his idea will have impact on receiver and what skill he should apply to have positive impact.

3. The sender encodes idea into message

Encoding is the process by which the sender converts his ideas into a message by using verbal and non-verbal mediums of communication. These can be words, signs, signals, gestures, symbols or body movement. The conversion of idea into a message connects the sender and receiver. In order to ensure that the messages will be understood the sender uses words and non-verbal signals that the receiver is familiar with. If not messages are rejected. Therefore skilled communicators pay attention to every detail of message composition.

4. The message travels through channel

Channel is the vehicle that carries the message to the receiver. The various channel include computer, fax, letter, telephone, report, picture, TV, radio, book etc. It is important for the senders to select appropriate channel suiting to the message. The choice of channel needs consideration of availability, preference, cost and quickness in delivering the message.

5. Noise in the channel

Anything that disrupts or interferes with the transmission process is called noise or barrier of communication. Channel noises can cause disturbances in the telephone, computer, television, radio, or error in typography. Sometimes unclear pronunciation in oral communication poor facial expression, poor gesture also creates barrier in communication. Poor selection of channel fort the message leads to failure of communication.

6. The receiver of the message

The receiver is any individual to whom message has been transmitted. Like sender the receiver has also attitude, values, ideas, opinions, beliefs' feelings and culture. The success and failure of communication also depends on how the receiver has perception about the message.

7. The receiver decodes the message

Decoding is the process of translating words, signs, symbols into meaning. Successful decoding is correct understanding of the intent of the message as transmitted by the sender. No communication can be completely successful or completely understood because no two persons are same.

8. Feedback sent by the receiver

The feedback is the receiver's response to the sender's message. The response can be verbal and non-verbal. It is an important factor in the communication process because it helps the sender to know whether message has been understood or not. Feedback demands great attention from the receiver of the message. Good listening skill, ability to read between the lines and interpret are required qualities of good receivers. Therefore communication is two way process. Both sender and receiver have equal responsibility to make communication a success.

9. Frame of reference of sender and receiver

Frame of reference is the combination of ideas, beliefs, opinion, attitude values, knowledge, culture, past experience and many other elements. Successful communication takes place when the sender's frame of reference matches the reciver's and vice-versa. The biggest challenge that sender faces is in drawing the receiver into his or her frame of reference.

10. The context of communication

Every communication takes place in a context. Context is formed by the combination of circumstances that influence the piece of communication at certain point of time. The influencing factors are physical surrounding, emotions, and their attitude & opinion. The context influence both encoding and decoding stage.

3

Verbal Communication How to Make it Effective

3.1. Types of communication network

There are different situations in which different kind of communication is required for transfer of technology. An Extension expert works in an organization. The organization demands communication of different types. These are:

1. Upward communication
2. Downward communication
3. Horizontal communication
5. Grapevine communication
6. External form of communication

1. Upward communication

Upward Communication is the process of information flowing from the lower levels of a hierarchy to the upper levels. This type of communication is becoming more popular in organizations as traditional forms of communication are becoming less popular.

2. Downward communication

The flow of information from higher levels of management to subordinate individuals working within an organization. The higher level officers make downward communication to motivate their staff to work better.

3. Horizontal communication

Horizontal communication refers to the flow of messages across functional areas on the same level of an organization. Effective use of horizontal communication in the workplace can enhance productivity by making information sharing, problem solving, collaboration, and conflict resolution more efficient.

4. Grapevine communication

Grapevine is an informal channel of business communication. It is called so because it stretches throughout the organization in all directions irrespective of the authority levels. Man as we know is a social animal

3.2 Use of Seven Cs of communication

The powerful seven Cs of communication govern the composition of all our messages whether we speak or write. We cannot escape their influence They are :

1. Courtesy
2. Clarity
3. Consciousness
4. Concreteness
5. Correctness
6. Consideration
7. Completeness

1. Courtesy

As word suggest the sender and receiver should have respect for each other. They should know the feeling of each other for good communication. In transfer of technology we not only want to transmit information but also create good will and harmonious relation. The relation between Extension expert and farmer is to be a living relationship. Then only communicated messages are accepted, understood and put to action. There are certain tips to maintain courtesy.

1. Be sincere
2. Avoid anger
3. Refrain from preaching
4. Use positive words
5. Avoid negative words
6. Never use discriminating words

2. Clarity

It is desirable to select simple, precise, familiar right words and short sentences to convey ideas or thoughts. It is more required in case of technology that is to be transferred. It is more required in case of transfer of farm technology to the farmers. The speaker or writer must know what kind of words the receiver will accept. The encoded message has mirror effect on the receiver. The factors that reduce clarity in verbal communication are:

1. Use of camouflage words
2. Use of passive voice
3. Use of long, convoluted style of writing
4. Use of rubber stamp words
5. Use of unfamiliar words

Messages that are not clear, have double meaning, ambiguous can result in waste of time and rejection of ideas.

3. Consciousness

This is prerequisite for effective communication. Clear communication is an inner driven focus to grow strong, mutually enriching relationships. Like giving and receiving, the effects of how you talk are inseparable from how you listen. They are intricately connected. Conscious-talking, however, is only half the equation in effective communication; the other half has to do with conscious-listening. The long widening message is the time killer and receivers reject such communication. Better to communicate with consciousness. Only relevant words and phrases are permitted in consciousness.

4. Concreteness

Clarity and consciousness come with use of concrete words. Use of figure, facts, names, example and vivid nouns add a special touch to expression. It helps to remember message. In communication of technology this is of special importance.

Concreteness is an aspect of communication that means being specific, definite, and vivid rather than vague and general. A concrete communication uses specific facts and figures. Concreteness is often taught in college communication courses as one of the aspects of effective communication.

It means message should be specific instead of general. Misunderstanding of words create problem for both sender and receiver. Better to use facts and figures instead of generic or irrevalent information.

5. Correctness

Correct use of grammer, message composition and appropriate words and adapting right level of communication to sit receiver's level determines the correctness of communication. Adapting right tone for conveying a message is basic to successful communication.

6. Consideration

It implies that the sender of the message gives due importance to the receiver and composes message keeping in mind requirement.

Consideration implies "stepping into the shoes of others". Effective communication must take the audience into consideration, i.e., the audience's view points, background, mind-set, education level, etc.

7. Completeness

The communication must be complete. It should convey all facts required by the audience. The sender of the message must take into consideration the receiver's mind set and convey the message accordingly. A complete communication has following features. It leaves no questions in the mind of receiver.

The completeness principle is a property of the real numbers, and is one of the foundations of real analysis.

3.3 Fidelity of communication

It is the degree of correspondence between the meaning intended by the sender of a message and the meaning understood by its receiver.

Fidelity is the quality of faithfulness or loyalty. Its original meaning regarded duty in a broader sense than the related concept of fealty. Both derive from the Latin word fidelity is, meaning "faithful or loyal".

Every communicator wants that his message should reach the audience with expression that he wants to convey. In other words we call it communication fidelity. Fidelity means that express meaning of the source perfectly and that translate message for receiver with complete accuracy.

Factors of communication fidelity (Berlo)

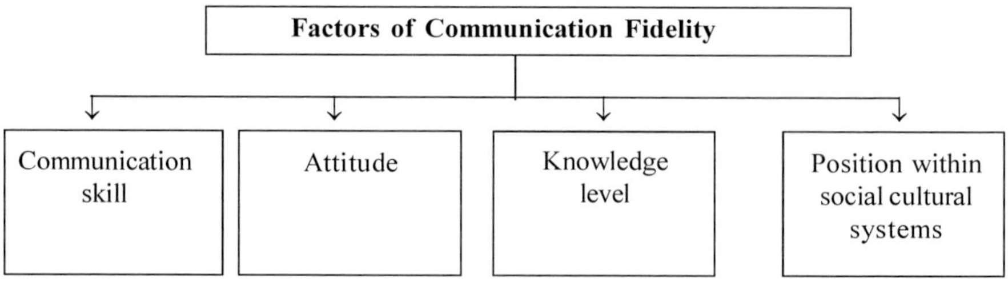

1. Communication skill

The communication skills we talk of are equally applicable to both sender and receiver of the message. These are:

1. Encoding skill: Writing and speaking

Encoding is the process of using letter/sound knowledge to write. If a student were to write that same sentence, instead of making sense of the letters in text, it is necessary to recall sounds and the symbols assigned to them to write the letters together to form word.

2. Decoding skill: Reading and listening

Decoding skills are the tools needed to make sense of the spoken or written word. These skills are necessary in order to read, write and speak. The word decoding commonly refers to understanding on the word level and not comprehension of higher meaning.

3. Both encoding and decoding: Reasoning

There are four basic forms of logic: deductive, inductive, adductive and metaphoric inference. In deduction inference leads from true propositions to true propositions.

Communication skill leads to fidelity in two ways

i) Affect our ability to analyze purpose, intention when we communicate

ii) Ability to encode message which expresses what we intend

2. Attitude

Attitude of the communicator affects his effectiveness. When the reader and listeners realize that writer or speaker like them, the message is likely to be accepted. The receiver feels the feeling of the sender of the massage. In short the attitude towards self and towards receiver decides the credibility of the source or sender.

3. Knowledge

One cannot communicate what one does not know. Knowledge about the message helps to communicate perfectly. Specialization on the subject enables the source to communicate more effectively. The source should have knowledge

1. About his own attitude
2. Characteristic of receiver
3. Ways he can produce message
4. Channel that carry the message

All these add to credibility of the sender of the message.

4. Position in socio-cultural system

The position of the source in socio-cultural system affect the communication behaviour, we need to know the kind of social system in which he lives and operates and people attach importance to him. The role he fulfils, functions he is required to perform, the prestige people attach to him all these affect communication behaviour.

3.4. Empathy

In the communication process the word' "Empathy" has special place.

When you have empathy, it means you can understand what a person is feeling in a given moment, and understand why other people's actions made sense to them. Empathy helps us to communicate our ideas in a way that makes sense to others, and it helps us understand others

Empathy is the ability to project oneself into other people's personality. It is the anticipation about audience. Normally before talking to someone , we first evaluate his personality or anticipate his feeling and then talk. Empathy comes from Germany word "Einfullung". The word was coined by Theodore Lipp in 1909. He did this to denote phenomena of perceiving other's behaviour or feeling as Einfullung and its meaning in English is narrowed down. Lipp originally intended to term to denote a process in which an individual observes gesture of another, imitates a previously experienced feeling and then projected feeling to the other persons. Later usages of the term "Empathy" contained a narrower meaning than intended by Lipp. But still it emphasizes feeling into other's emotion.

3.4.1 Definitions of empathy

i) Roger and Svening. Empathy is defined as ability of an individual to project himself into the role of another person.

ii) H.C.Smith. The core idea of empathy is the ability to transpose oneself imaginatively into the feelings, thinking and acting of another.

iii) Berlo. Empathy can be defined as process through which we arrive at expectation, anticipation of the internal psychological status of a man

iv) Allopert and Strunk. Role taking or putting oneself in other fellow's play was constantly present in all the definitions of empathy.

3.4.2 Types of empathy

The Empathy is of two types

i) Source's empathy: Empathises his audience which saves his own communication. If the source empathises his audience his communication becomes effective

ii) Receiver's empathy: Likewise empathy of receiver for source increases effectiveness of his communication.

4

Non-Verbal Communication

4.1 The non-verbal communication

The non-verbal communication is the use of human body as the medium of message. The non-verbal communication forms a vital part of the process of communication that an individual goes through daily. *Non-verbal communication* is communication that does not involve words, such as body language, tone of voice, and gestures. Nonverbal communication is the transfer of information through the use of body language including eye contact, facial expressions, gestures and more. Verbal communication is the use of language to transfer information through written text, speaking or sign language.

Non Verbal Communication can play five roles

1. **Repetition:** It repeats and often strengthens the message you're making verbally.
2. **Contradiction:** It can contradict the message you're trying to convey, thus indicating to your listener that you may not be telling the truth.
3. **Substitution:** It can substitute for a verbal message. For example, your facial expression often conveys a far more vivid message than words ever can.
4. **Complementing:** It may add to or complement your verbal message. As a boss, if you pat an employee on the back in addition to giving praise, it can increase the impact of your message.
5. **Accenting:** It may accent or underline a verbal message. Pounding the table, for example, can underline the importance of your message.

4.2 Types of non-verbal communication

The many different types of non-verbal communication or body language include:

1. **Facial expressions:** The human face is extremely expressive, able to convey countless emotions without saying a word. And unlike some forms of nonverbal communication, facial expressions are universal. The facial expressions for happiness, sadness, anger, surprise, fear, and disgust are the same across cultures.

2. **Body movement and posture:** Consider how your perceptions of people are affected by the way they sit, walk, stand, or hold their head. The way you move and carry yourself communicates a wealth of information to the world. This type of nonverbal communication includes your posture, bearing, stance, and the subtle movements you make.
3. **Gestures:** Gestures are woven into the fabric of our daily lives. You may wave, point, beckon, or use your hands when arguing or speaking animatedly, often expressing yourself with gestures without thinking. However, the meaning of some gestures can be very different across cultures. While the OK sign made with the hand, for example, conveys a positive message in English-speaking countries, it's considered offensive in countries such as Germany, Russia, and Brazil. So, it's important to be careful of how you use gestures to avoid misinterpretation.
4. **Eye contact:** Since the visual sense is dominant for most people, eye contact is an especially important type of nonverbal communication. The way you look at someone can communicate many things, including interest, affection, hostility, or attraction. Eye contact is also important in maintaining the flow of conversation and for gauging the other person's interest and response.
5. **Touch:** We communicate a great deal through touch. Think about the very different messages given by a weak handshake, a warm bear hug, a patronizing pat on the head, or a controlling grip on the arm, for example.
6. **Space:** Have you ever felt uncomfortable during a conversation because the other person was standing too close and invading your space? We all have a need for physical space, although that need differs depending on the culture, the situation, and the closeness of the relationship. You can use physical space to communicate many different nonverbal messages, including signals of intimacy and affection, aggression or dominance.
7. **Voice:** It's not just what you say, it's ***how*** you say it. When you speak, other people "read" your voice in addition to listening to your words. Things they pay attention to include your timing and pace, how loud you speak, your tone and inflection, and sound that convey understanding, such as "ahh" and "uh-huh." Think about how your tone of voice can indicate sarcasm, anger, affection, or confidence.

4.3 Use of body languages

A lot of literatures are available on body language. Research on it reveals the gestural communication in terms of prominent ones like use of body languages in interview, social meets, training program etc.

I. Understanding Body Language and Facial Expressions (Kendra Cherry.2019)

II. Cheery (2019) has dealt with non verbal communication citing examples.

III. According to him the facial expression is one of the strong body language in communication.

1. Facial Expression

Face indicates the position of sender while communicating the message. A smile can indicate approval or happiness. A frown can signal disapproval or unhappiness.

In some cases, our facial expressions may reveal our true feelings about a particular situation. While we say that we are feeling fine the face indicates it in true form.

Just a few examples of emotions that can be expressed via facial expressions include:

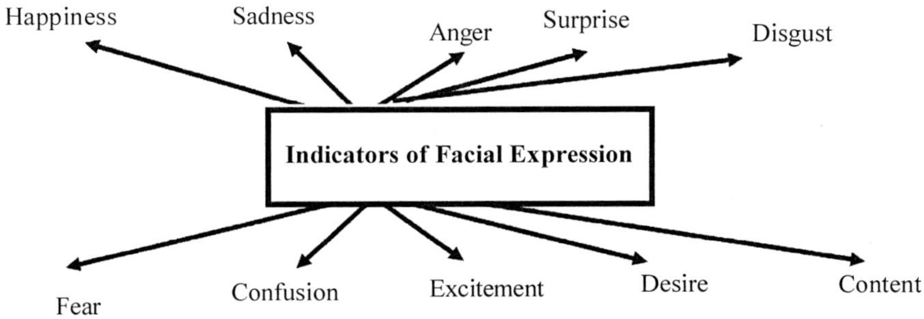

The expression on a person's face can even help determine if we trust or believe what the individual is saying.

One study found that the most trustworthy facial expression involved a slight raise of the eyebrows and a slight smile. This expression, the researchers suggested, conveys both friendliness and confidence.

Facial expressions are also among the most universal forms of body language. The expressions used to convey fear, anger, sadness, and happiness are similar throughout the world.

Research even suggests that we make judgments about people's intelligence based upon their faces and expressions.

One study found that individuals who had narrower faces and more prominent noses were more likely to be perceived as intelligent. People with smiling, joyful expression were also judged as being more intelligent than those with angry expressions.

2. The Eyes

The eyes are frequently referred to as the "windows to the soul" since they are capable of revealing a great deal about what a person is feeling or thinking.

When one is engaged in conversation with another person, eye movements reveal natural and important part of the communication process.

3. Eye Gaze

When a person looks directly into eyes of other while having a conversation, it indicates that they are interested and paying attention. However, prolonged eye contact can feel threatening.

On the other hand, breaking eye contact and frequently looking away might indicate that the person is distracted, uncomfortable, or trying to conceal his or her real feelings.

4. Blinking

Blinking is natural, but we have to pay attention to whether a person is blinking too much or too little.

People often blink more rapidly when they are feeling distressed or uncomfortable. Infrequent blinking may indicate that a person is intentionally trying to control his or her eye movements.

5. Pupil Size

Pupil size can be a very subtle nonverbal communication signal. While light levels in the environment control pupil dilation, sometimes emotions can also cause small changes in pupil size.

6. The Mouth

Mouth expressions and movements can also be essential in reading body language. For example, chewing on the bottom lip may indicate that the individual is experiencing feelings of worry, fear, or insecurity.

Covering the mouth may be an effort to be polite if the person is yawning or coughing, but it may also be an attempt to cover up a frown of disapproval. Smiling is perhaps one of the greatest body language signals, but smiles can also be interpreted in many ways.

A smile may be genuine, or it may be used to express false happiness, sarcasm, or even cynicism.

When evaluating body language, pay attention to the following mouth and lip signals:

i) Pursed lips. Tightening the lips might be an indicator of distaste, disapproval, or distrust.

ii) Lip biting. People sometimes bite their lips when they are worried, anxious, or stressed.

iii) Covering the mouth. When people want to hide an emotional reaction, they might cover their mouths in order to avoid displaying smiles or smirks.

iv) Turned up or down. Slight changes in the mouth can also be subtle indicators of what a person is feeling. When the mouth is slightly turned up, it might mean that the person is feeling happy or optimistic. On the other hand, a slightly down-turned mouth can be an indicator of sadness, disapproval, or even an outright grimace.

7. Gestures

Gestures can be some of the most direct and obvious body language signals. Waving, pointing, and using the fingers to indicate numerical amounts are all very common and easy to understand gestures.

Some gestures may be cultural, however, so giving a thumbs-up or a peace sign in another country might have a completely different meaning than it does in the United States.

The following examples are just a few common gestures and their possible meanings:

i) A clenched fist can indicate anger in some situations or solidarity in others.

ii) A thumbs up and thumbs down are often used as gestures of approval and disapproval.

iii) The "okay" gesture, made by touching together the thumb and index finger in a circle while extending the other three fingers can be used to mean "okay" or "all right.

iv) The V sign created by lifting the index and middle finger and separating them to create a V-shape, means peace or victory in some countries. In the United Kingdom and Australia, the symbol takes on an offensive meaning when the back of the hand is facing outward.

8. The Arms and Legs

The arms and legs can also be useful in conveying nonverbal information. Crossing the arms can indicate defensiveness. Crossing legs away from another person may indicate dislike or discomfort with that individual.

Other subtle signals such as expanding the arms widely may be an attempt to seem larger or more commanding while keeping the arms close to the body may be an effort to minimize oneself or withdraw from attention.

On evaluating body language, we have to pay attention to some of the following signals that the arms and legs may convey.

1. Crossed arms might indicate that a person feels defensive, self-protective, or closed-off.
2 Standing with hands placed on the hips can be an indication that a person is ready and in control, or it can also possibly be a sign of aggressiveness.
3. Clasping the hands behind the back might indicate that a person is feeling bored, anxious, or even angry
4 Rapidly tapping fingers or fidgeting can be a sign that a person is bored, impatient, or frustrated
5 Crossed legs can indicate that a person is feeling closed off or in need of privacy.

9. Posture

How we hold our bodies can also serve as an important part of body language.

The term *posture* refers to how we hold our bodies as well as the overall physical form of an individual.

Posture can convey a wealth of information about how a person is feeling as well as hints about personality characteristics, such as whether a person is confident, open, or submissive.

i) Sitting up straight, for example, may indicate that a person is focused and paying attention to what's going on. Sitting with the body hunched forward, on the other hand, can imply that the person is bored or indifferent.

   The signals that a person's posture can send.

ii) Open posture involves keeping the trunk of the body open and exposed. This type of posture indicates friendliness, openness, and willingness.

ii) Closed posture involves hiding the trunk of the body often by hunching forward and keeping the arms and legs crossed. This type of posture can be an indicator of hostility, unfriendliness, and anxiety.

10. Personal Space

The term *proxemics*, coined by anthropologist Edward T. Hall, refers to the distance between people as they interact. Just as body movements and facial expressions can communicate a great deal of nonverbal information, so can the physical space between individuals.

Hall described four levels of social distance that occur in different situations.

S. No.	Distance	Meaning
1.	Intimate Distance: 6 to 18 inches	This level of physical distance often indicates a closer relationship or greater comfort between individuals. It usually occurs during intimate contact such as hugging, whispering, or touching
2.	Personal Distance: 1.5 to 4 feet	Physical distance at this level usually occurs between people who are family members or close friends. The closer the people can comfortably stand while interacting can be an indicator of the level of intimacy in their relationship
3.	Social Distance: 4 to 12 feet.	This level of physical distance is often used with individuals who are acquaintances.
4.	Public Distance: 12 to 25 feet	Physical distance at this level is often used in public speaking situations. Talking in front of a class full of students or giving a presentation at work are good examples of such situations

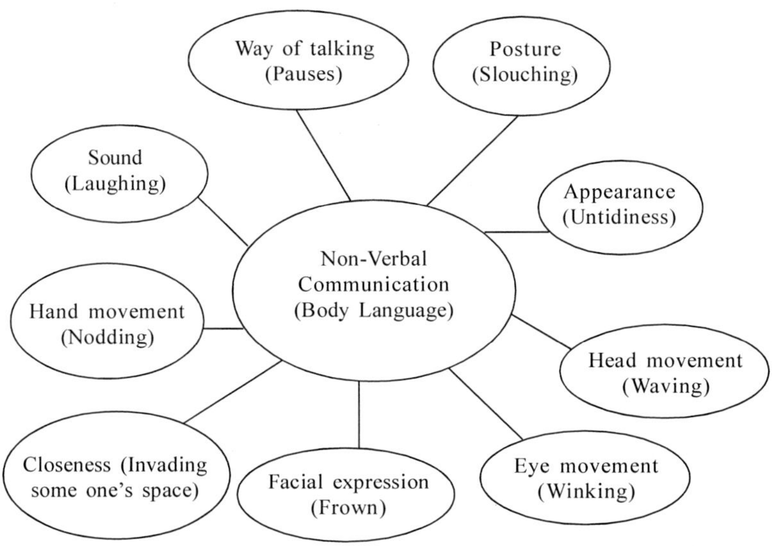

Non-Verbal Communication

5

Listening

5.1 A great deal of research

A great deal of research has been carried out on listening in communication. According to the researchers, listening comes at top of the list of the four forms of communication

1. Listening
2. Speaking
3. Writing
4. Reading

There are some misconceptions about learning. For both sender and receiver good listening is important to keep communication process active. The misconceptions are:

5.1.1. Listening is same as hearing

Hearing is a passive activity while listening is active. Listening is ot automatic like hearing. In hearing the sound waves strike eardrum causing vibration. These are then transmitted to brain. Listening occurs only when the brain swing to action by restructuring these 'electrochemical 'impulses by giving meaning to the sound.

5.1.2 Listening is same thing as breathing

Breathing is a continuous process. Listening is not. Listening is a continuous process like deep breathing and not a passive one. In a seminar or conference the audience do not listen equally. Some respond while some do not to the question raised. It implies that listening is passive for those do not respond. Therefore active listening is not hearing as we feel. Further sleeping in seminar is an example of hearing but not listening.

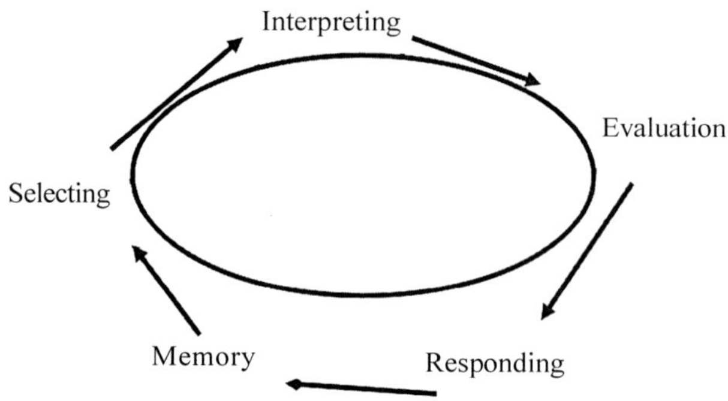

5.2 Stages of listening

There are five important stages in the process of listening.

1. Sensing/selecting stage

The listener selects from among multiple stimuli only one that seems important at that point of time and converts it into message.

2. Interpreting stage

The listener is engaged in the act of decoding the message. At this stage listener is faces with multiple barriers i.e. semantic may be linguistic, psychological, emotional or environmental.

3. Evaluating stage

At this stage the listener assigns meaning to the message, draws inferences, takes an over view of the message and seeks accuracy of information and evidences. At this stage the listener may be disturbed by previous experience, bleifs, & emotion. Therefore the listener evaluates the message to reply or not.

4. Responding stage

At this stage the listener is ready to reply. This is feedback stage. The listener's non-verbal signals tell the sender whether he is understood or not.

5. Memory stage

This is the final stage of learning. Effective listening help the listener to retain chunk of what he has listened. Memorability is an important index for the listener to test how much he has stored in memory bank.

5.3 Benefits of effective learning

1. Improvement in work environment

Proactive listeners always make it a point to understand the real meaning of the message that are transmitted increasingly. This they do by discovering the sender's beliefs, values and sense of commitment, expectation and goal. Good listening is conducive to efficient work.

2. Reduce tensions and hostiles

Positive listening establishes a wider and flexible frame of reference so that people are willing in the act of listening. This paves for healthy exchange of views and opinions thus reduce possibility of psychological tension.

3. Saves time

Good listeners are always time conscious and concerned about how the materials can be used for the benefit of organization

4. Improves relation

Open door policy reaffirms employee's faith and trust in the management. The people enjoy the freedom to express their grievances a feeling of positive attitude.

5. Leads to early problem solving

Good listening helps to detect and solve problems earlier because of good understanding, clarification of doubt and clear understanding.

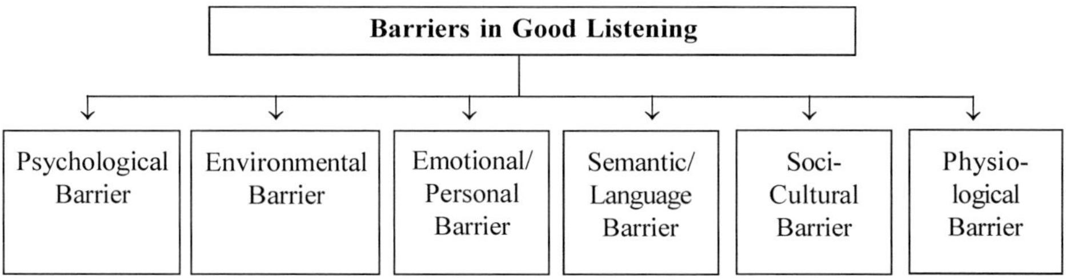

5.4. Barriers in good listening

1. Psychological barrier

There are seven psychological barriers in good listening

i) **Prejudgement and hasty evaluation:** Without listening completely some draw wrong conclusions. The listener passes a hasty unfounded remark about the sender.

ii) **Superficial frame of reference:** Without listening correctly listener draws a wrong conclusion. He judges speaker on own back ground and thus learns very little and may be contained with wrong information. These are superficial listeners who blame the sender quickly without any fact.

iii) **Close-mindedness :** Some listeners close their minds before listening fully and thus spread wrong message.

iv) **Inability to pay attention :** A wandering and day dreaming habit prevents the listeners to listen the message completely.

v) **Prejudice:** The personal limitation like hatred towards speaker also acts as barrier to good listening.

vi) **Ego:** Some listeners due to their ego do not listen to speaker sincerely.

2. Environmental factors

i) **Physical distraction:** Noise surrounding, loud music, noise of machine, sound of vehicle creates obstruction.

ii) **Loud talking:** Loud voice of people in congregation, conversation create barrier in listening

iii) **Visual barrier:** Visuals like picture, dress, jewellery etc. create barrier in listening.

3. Emotional barrier

i) **Belief and attitude:** Belief and attitude towards speaker decide extent of listening.

ii) **Sad memories:** A reference to sad memory also debars the listeners to listen

iii) **Fear:** Sometimes fear act as barrier in listening to those who are opposed in society.

iv) **Anxiety:** Sometimes health and mind being on anxiety prevent listening.

v) **Anger:** Anger does not allow to listen speaker because of past event

4. Linguistic /Semantic barrier

The following semantic problems act as barrier in listening

i) Speaker's style of speaking and manner

ii) Difficult words

iii) Long time

iv) Different frame of reference than the topic

v) Use of double meaning words

5. Socio-Cultural barriers

Three important factors create problem in listening

i) Different cultural back ground

ii) Personal space and public space

iii) Sense of time

6. Physiological barrier

i) Hearing impairment or disability

ii) Hungry stomach may not allow listening more

iii) Tiredness due to over work

iv) Physical body pain does not allow listening.

5.5 Factors not promoting good listening

1. Declare that subject is not interesting
2. Criticize content of speech
3. Criticize the speaker's manner of speaking
4. Pretend to be attentive
5. Jumping to conclusion

6

Writing for Farmers

The extension professionals are interested to disseminate technology to the users. The users are rural people. The users of technology are to read and understand technology designed for them. Rural readers have different interests like, crop production, animal husbandry, fisheries, forestry etc. They need technologies in these fields to increase production and productivity. Farm related articles are to be published in news papers and farm magazines in local language. There are certain points that need to be taken care while writing for rural readers.

6.1. Writing for rural readers

Rural readers are normally acquainted in local language. They prefer to talk and listen in their day to day language. Farm journalism wishes to push technical information to rural population. The rural readers will search and select the literature suiting to their understanding. Therefore writing for rural readers needs special skill.

Requirements for such writings are

1. **Lucidity of Language**: Language should be simple, conspicuous and lucid. Readers if find difficult in language will stop reading. Lucidity of language is the core skill for writing of farm related articles.
2. **Issues in writing:** To make good writing, one has to underline the need of narrative approach with emphasis on (i) simple word (ii) short sentence (iii) one thought (iv) active voice. These ingredients in writing receive interest and attention of the readers.
3. **Jargons of words:** Rural readers need familiar words. We want to induce technical words. A search of familiar words to express technical words is rewarding all the times. Therefore better to avoid repletion of ideas, jargons and unfamiliar words as far as possible. Where technical words have no substitutions, we have to use them but in an understanding manner suiting to the understanding level of the readers.
4. **Prominence of issues**: The issues that we want our readers should go through should be prominently written and other issues to be avoided as far as possible.

5. **Illustrations: Figures, illustrations.** The relevant illustrations, figures, sketches are to be given with to explain points. Special attention is to be given to place illustrations side by side of the points or action to be explained.

6.2 Interest to write for farmers

Very people show interest to write for farmers of country side. The reasons are, (i) not having appreciation for rural readers (ii) not able to write technical issues in local language (iii) lack of recognition and (iv) not good in business. But those are the students of rural development faculties or agriculture and allied colleges they should have interest to write for farmers. This is so because they have to work with farmers after completion of their professional education. Farm news or journals are good medium to disseminate technological information.

At post graduate level in the discipline of Extension Education farm journalism is offered as course. We expect the students undergoing the course should develop habit of writing for farm families. The result of a reported study shows that hardly 5-8% of extension students like to write for farmers. To increase interest among writers there is need to increase number of farm magazines with greater frequencies.

Guidelines of Farm Journlism

1. Use simple language	Technical terms in simple, short and use of common words
2. Clear the structure	Ideas in logical order
3. Make points brief	Main points, brief and short
4. Use of lively pictures and photographs	Photo in action, good construct, good composition
5. Keep important information at top	Important message at top
6. Stimulating	Interesting, inspiring, personal, diversified

Tips of writing farm articles

1. Facts to be written should be brief, but key points are to be kept.
2. Purpose of writing to be very clear like, only to inform or farmers have to take action.
3. Content of article should by understandable by majority of the readers.
4. Mention that why the article is written and what is expected from readers.
5. Article should contain accurate fact in clear term. The readers should not get wrong message
6. Write to express the idea.
7. The words should be conventional or familiars with readers.

8. Good farm related articles are devoid of jargon and difficult technical terms.
9. Short sentence composed of 15-18 words have relatively more impact
10. Good paragraph should not contain more than five sentences.
11. Articles written for rural readers on technological issues should be composed of short sentence
12. Use of active voice is must as it has relatively more force.
13. Use of standard punctuation, spelling and grammar
14. Good writers are conscious of neat and legibility
15. Maintaining of consistency in usages of tense, mood, voice, verb and one subject keeps attention of readers on the topic of the article.
16. Repetition of same words makes writing dull.
17. Use active verb in present tense to make writing attractive. Avoid words like, will, will be, and must.

6.3 Steps in writing articles

Writing of article is a skill. One has to acquire it for good writing. Everybody likes to write. The technical writing is different than other writing. While dealing with farming communities the extension professionals write for their clients who are heterogeneous in the behaviour according to their livelihood system. There are six recognized steps in writing which the writers ought to follow.

Six Steps in Writing Articles

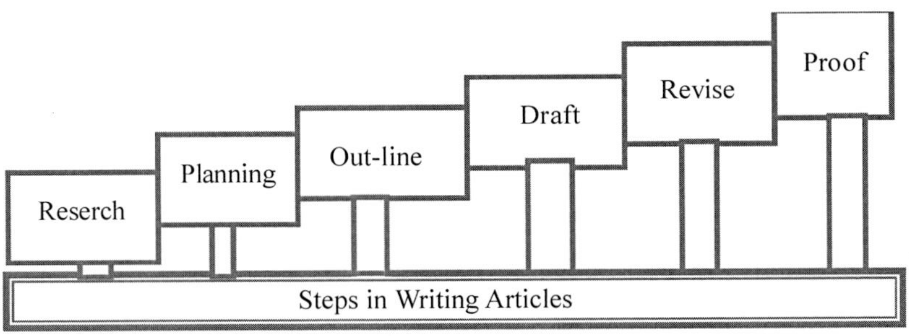

I. **Research**: Research in article writing is the search after technology that audience need. Making a thorough brainstorming the writer has to decide the need of article.

Once the issues for article are determined then writer has to contact the research stations for content or exact message that are to be in article. The sources of research contents are, (i) ICAR institutes, (II) Agriculture university (iii) KVKs

(iv) private research institutes etc. At this stage the writer has to make an exercise on the following aspects.

1. Decide the topic for article
2. On a rough paper write down all the points relating to topic.
3. Indicate the focus of the topic
4. Keep in mind that who are the readers of the article
5. Have look to the points and segregate the unrelated ideas in relation to topic and remove them.
6. Now group the ideas in relation to each other
7. Eliminate the group not supporting ideas
8. Decide headline for each group
9. Prepare outline of the article
10. Verify the appropriateness of each heading and ideas under it.

II. **Planning for writing article:** While planning to write an article for rural audience two major aspects are to be considered. These are,

1. Basic questions to be considered
2. Parts of the planning of an article

Basic questions in planning for article

Four wives and one husband

1. Who
2. Where
3. What
4. Where
5. How

1. **WHO:** 'WHO' is an important question to be considered first? **Who** needs answer on the following points?

   Who intends to find answer to,

1. Who are the receivers of the message?
2. What are the problems they face and through message we want to solve.
3. What are basic ideas of the readers about the issue?
4. What are their educational back ground, as well as social, economical and cultural back ground?
5. Whether they have means to take action on suggested measures.

While recognize 'who' of writing there is need to know (i) responsibility of audience (ii) purpose of reading the article (iii) their perception about topic (iv) educational back ground and (v) their experience

Types of audience: Use of 5W and 1 H is very much essential in farm writing. We studied use of these in farm journal published in Odisha.

Types of audience

General	Decision maker	Farm Operator	Experts
1. Non specific	1. Deals with cost, personal, productivity, market	1. Variation in experience	1. Fully aware of procedure
2. Lack of technical experience	2. Need bottom line information and conclusion	2. Manufactirers	2. Need adequate data for support
3. Needs to be informed, persuaded, entertained		3. Need step by step procedure	3. Knowlgeable in line

2. **WHERE:** The "where" implies to know in which location the technical message can be put into action. In others words, the article is written for people of which locality. The use of message in those locations in relation to agro climatic zone, people's preference, market for produce and interest of the readers are to be ascertained.
3. **WHAT:** The 'What' of writing needs careful consideration of the Points like:

1. Accuracy of facts
2. Relation between facts and solution of problem
3. Central theme
4. Weighing of facts
5. Timeliness of article
6. Meeting the needs of readers.
7. Affordability of readers

4. **WHY:** The why reason of writing. The question is very pertinent for writer. Under "why" the questions are:

1. What is the purpose?
2. What result the publication will achieve?
3. Is it meant for stimulating readers for program?

4. It is meant for informing people about the skill of doing a thing?
5. What response is expected from the readers?
6. What kind of feedback is expected?

5. **WHEN:** It means when the readers are going to use the content or message. The time of use of message and writing of related article is an important factor to be kept in mind.
6. **HOW**: How to write and outline of article can be achieved through a thorough brain-storming. Think again and again and then draw an outline of article.

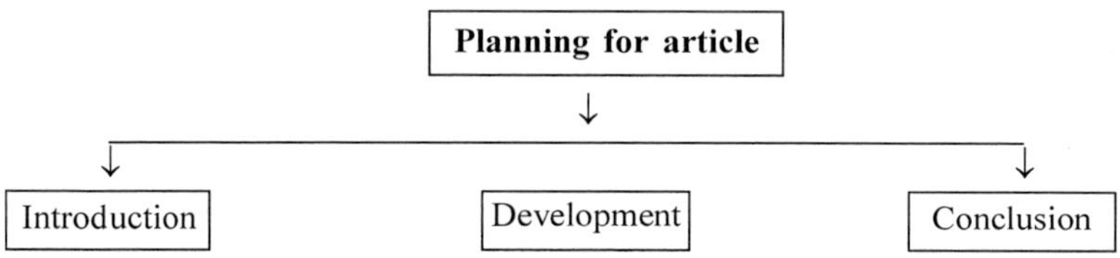

I. Introduction

1. Start forming outline of article
2. Start from bottom line: Collect Ideas and group them in sequence.

   Bottom line should not carry more than three ideas.
3. Bottom line relevant to purpose of writing
4. Content is focus on single idea
5. Information given should support bottom line
6. Sequence of parts in an article makes writing more effective
7. Final consistency of the given materials
8. Leading from bottom line to major part and subordinate part

II. Development style

1. Time to be chronological in order
2. Space to be spatial in order
3. General to particular point
4. Particular to general point
5. Advantage and disadvantage
6. Break down to part and analyze
7. Cause and effect relationship

III. Closing

1. Suggestion for action
2. Reward for achievement
3. **Outline of Article**: The outline is the frame within one has to keep writing limited. It is to be thought well and planned. Different parameters of good outline are illustrated here.

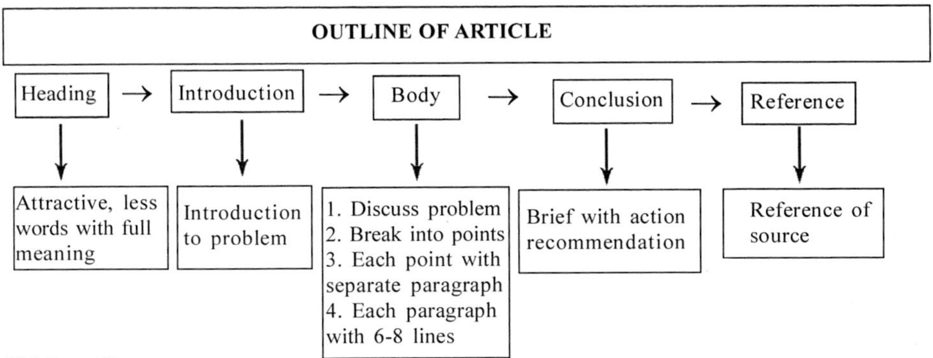

IV. Draft

While preparing draft, the writer has to remember the followings

1. Choose best format and packaging and organize them properly
2. Good packaging for smooth reading

Packaging means inclusion of

1. Heading
2. Tables
3. Underlining
4. Highlighting
5. Bold letters
6. Capital letters
7. Italic
8. Colour
9. Column

Steps in Draft

In article writing better to follow three specific steps in making draft. They are called, 1st draft 2nd draft and 3rd draft. Some authors advice the drafting in five steps.

1st **Draft:** While making first draft the writer may look to the following points and assign percentage against each. By this process he can decide to retain/ remove/modify the draft.

Initial draft checking

Content	% of satisfaction of the writer	Retain/Delete/Modify
1. Need of the text		
2. Appropriateness of contents of sections		
3. Sequence of paragraph		
4. Need for division require of paragraph		
5. Appropriateness of headings and subheading to the section		
6. Informative, specificity and conciseness of title		
7. Inclusion of all elements in abstract		
8. Appropriateness of table and figures		
9. Foot note, table heading and figure legends whether appropriate		
10. Acknowledgement of assistance received		
11. Reference checking with original		
12. Mention of reference in the text		

2nd **Draft:** Second draft needs the process of refinement. Refinement can be achieved through criticism by appropriate readers. Appropriate readers means having knowledge on the subject of the article.

3rd **Draft**: At this stage only correctness and review of article are done. Writer himself can look to these

V. Revise

Substance, Organization, style, correctness

Relevancy of Document

Sequence and organization of
1. Introduction
2. Development
3. Conclusion

Style of writting
1. Bottom line
2. Unty
3. Coherence
4. Paragraph Coherence
5. Sentence Coherence
6. Emphasis
7. Conclusion

VI. Proof reading

Check and mark the final copy. Always it should be checked by somebody else to detect mistake than the writer himself.

VII. Conclusion

THINK, PLAN, WRITE and REWRITE

Skilful writing is an art and it needs good preparation.

The writings for farmers do not become attractive and effective because writers do not pay due attention to the specific steps that could improve the quality of writing.

6.4 Examine your own biases

i) Periodically examine yourself for bias building up — understanding what your views are and why you have them is the best way to keep them under control.

ii) Who does you personally like or dislike? Why?

iii) How might that be colouring your judgment?

iv) Through some of your stories and be self-critical.

Good stories prove their relevance to the audience

People care most about things that affect them.

On one level, the relevance of a story can be a function of geography. The reader is more interested in his local weather forecast than the national outlook. He is more interested in knowing why a police officer is taking a report on his block than somewhere else in the city.

A different kind of proximity involves emotions or interests. The reader may identify with a range of life experiences, from the emotional shock of losing a job or worrying about a sick child to mundane tasks like the weekly trip to the grocery store or filling the car with gas. Readers also identify with their own special interests, whether a hobby or sport or an important pocketbook issues like taxes, interest rates, school quality, crime and safety, health care, or economic development.

6.5 News Story

News is written for information of public. For rural audience farm news are essentially required. Farm news is those which benefit only farmers living in rural areas. These are crop, seed, market, input, credit, Govt. policy, animal and fish related news. There may be more of such kind.

News is timely information that interests the readers. It should be accurate in fact and timely so that readers can be interested to read. It has more relevance in local news papers than national ones. To write for rural audience certain guidelines are followed to make news interesting. News is to :

i) Develop interest

ii) Inform general public

iii) Disseminate information and

iv) Creates favourable attitude.

What makes a good story?

A good story is about something the audience decides is interesting or important. A *great* story often does both by using storytelling to make important news interesting.

The public is exceptionally diverse. Though people may share certain characteristics or beliefs, they have an untold variety of concerns and interests.

So *anything can* be news. But not everything is *newsworthy*. Journalism is a process in which a reporter uses verification and storytelling to make a subject newsworthy.

At its most basic level, news is a function of distribution news organizations (or members of the public) creates stories to pass on a piece of information to readers, viewers, or listeners.

A good story, however, does more than inform or amplify. It adds value to the topic.

The Elements of Journalism

The elements of journalism have been topic of many authors who have expressed their differential views. In fact, the elements describe journalism as "storytelling with a purpose."

Creating a good story means finding and verifying important or interesting information and then presenting it in a way that engages the audience. Good stories are part of what make journalism different, and more valuable, than other content in the media universe.

Research proves two things about good stories:

i) **Treatment trumps topic.** How a story is told is more important to the audience than its topic, what it is about. The best story is a well-told tale about something the reader feels is relevant or significant.

ii) **The best stories are more complete and more comprehensive.** They contain more verified information from more sources with more viewpoints and expertise. They exhibit more enterprise, more reportorial effort.

How to organize a story

Often, when journalists approach an assignment, they start one of two ways:

i) One way is to read previous stories or check the Web, see what has been written before, and then add what's new on top, refreshing what's already been said.

ii) The other is to meet with an editor, develop a theme for the piece and pursue that, adding in the background from the earlier stories.

The problem with both of these approaches is that they can leave out the audience. If the purpose of journalism is to tell people what they need to know to navigate their way through their world, it follows then that journalists need to keep our audience in the forefront when making decisions about coverage. The tools in this section help you understand how to organize your stories.

6.6 Questions to find a focus for your story

Ask these questions during the editorial process: when planning a story, when doing the reporting and photography, when writing and editing, when deciding how to present it, and in determining if follow-up is warranted. What are the central point, evidence, place and character?

1. What is the central point?

a) What's the story really about? What question or questions must the story answer to be worthwhile?

b) Why does people need or will want to know about it?

c) If it's a "big" topic, how can it be broken down so it's easier to explain?

d) If it's a "small" topic, is there a story behind the story? Does it reflect a larger trend or theme?

2. What is the central evidence?

a) What kinds of evidence can be presented to verify or explain the central point of the story?

b) What kinds of evidence can be presented to prove that the story is relevant or newsworthy?

c) How good is the evidence? Will the reader be able to distinguish verified information from assumptions or assertions the story may also include?

3. What is the central place?

a) Where is the central place of the story?

b) Will the reporting and photography include covering the central place?

c) What information will come from somewhere other than the central place or places?

d) What will not be covered in the story?

4. Who are the central characters?

a) Where or from whom can the facts be learned?

b) Who can put the facts in perspective?

c) What is the relationship between the central characters and the central places of the story?

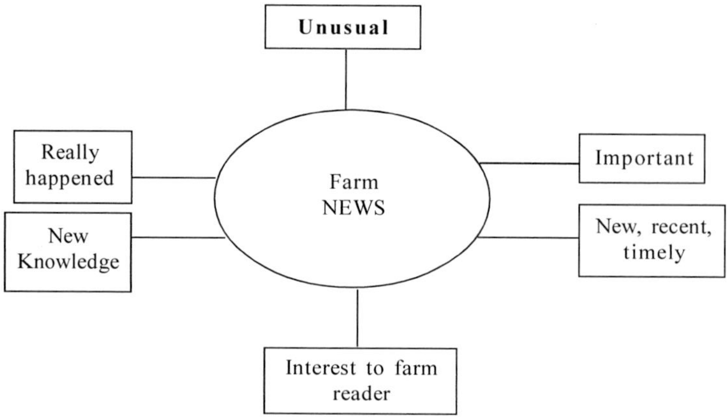

Characteristics of Good Farm News

Writing for rural audience needs special care because many of them are not up to-date on recent happening. Normally writers are interested for urban readers. Many authors have mentioned a number attributes for rural writing, News Stories are of special mention because of public demand and increasing importance of State and national governments. Writers always are interested as how to attract attention of readers to their news stories.

In the state of Odisha the farmers are residing in ten agro-climatic zones. Their farming system, occupation, farm business, market system etc. have some difference. Therefore either print media or electronic media should carry farm news accordingly. In other words it is a communication process in which source; receiver, channel and message are considered while preparing farm news. The communication process postulated by Wilbur Schramme is being considered to present quality message to the farmers and farming community.

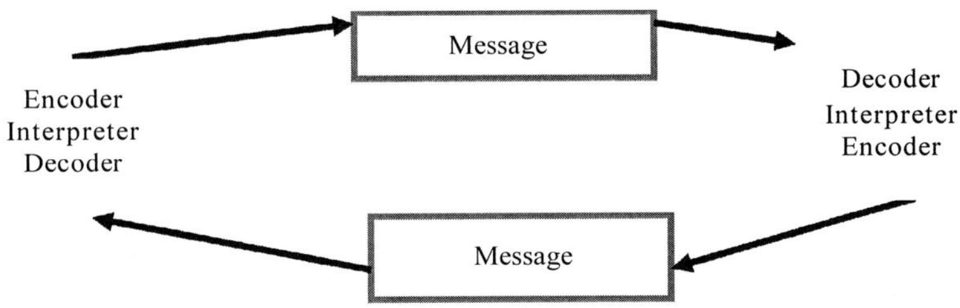

Schramme model of communication

Characteristics of Good Farm News

Several studies reveal that good farm news should have the following characteristics. These characteristics create interest for reading and lead to action in farm management operations.

1. Objectivity
2. Completeness
3. ABC, i.e. Accuracy, Brevity and Clarity
4. News in sequence
5. Principles of news writing
6. Follow inverted pyramid in writing
7. Short paragraph
8. Short photograph
9. Style of writing
10. Importance of news
11. Lead sentence
12. Devoid of personal matter
13. Use of 5 W and 1 H

Determinants of News Value

Normally the students of journalism ask the questions as what kind of news carries more value so that readers will be attracted to read. There has been a lot of study in this field. A study conducted in Odisha is presented here with to have insight to the topic

Determinants of news value

S.No.	Topic related to	Attention of readers (%)
1.	Uniqueness	15.00
2.	Impact	12.00
3.	Suspense	18.00
4.	Conflict	10.00
5.	Emotion	11.00
6.	Progress	14.00
7.	Surprise	12.00
8.	Sex	8.00

Determinants of NEWS value are many. Important out of them are,

1. Timeliness: Shortest period to reach people
2. Nearness or Proximity: Local events psychologically more attractive
3. Consequence: How information affect the common people
4. Human Interest: Related to human beings of greater interest
5 Prominence: Prominent people, place, event
6. Editorial policy: Good and unbiased editorial comment

6.7 Principles of writing news stories

News story writing is a special art. Before attempting to write news story, one has to learn the principle of writing it and should proceed accordingly. Some principles are cited here but not exclusive. An innovative mind can add much to it by asking questions which are related to principles.

1. What is specific purpose of writing, whether to inform, to educate or to entertain the readers.
2. Have full idea about people for whom writing is directed.
3. Know the subject on which the readers are interested.
4. Timely and immediate communication makes news important.
5. Simple and clear writing is must.
6. News must be well convincing

7. Exaggeration kills interest of the readers.
8. Use of personal words interests readers.
9. Select right, short words and avoid unusual words.
10. One idea approach in one sentence.
11. Short paragraph and short sentence adds value to writing.
12. Smooth transition from paragraph to paragraph
13. Specific points are keys to good news writing
14. Direct and meaningful quotations increase interest.
15. Honesty in reporting and writing is to be maintained.
16. Rumours are to be avoided at any cost
17. Past tense and active voice are to be used.
18. Make caption attractive
19. Avoid jargons and use simple terms
20. Lead paragraph should be attractive
21. News story should answer 5 W and 1 H

Primciples for Writing of news story for Rural Readers

→
1. Purpose
2. Knowledge about readers
3. Knowledge on Subject matter
4. Timely and immediate news

→
1. Simple and clear writing
2. Convincing
3. Absence of exaggeration
4. Use of personal words

→
1. Right words and short sentence
2. One sentence with one idea
3. Short paragraph and short sentence
4. Smooth transition from paragraph to

→
1. Specific points are key to good newswriting
2. Direct and meaningful quotations increase interest
3. Honesty in reporting and writing is to be maintained

→
1. Rumours are to be avoided at any cost
2. Past tense and active voice are to be used
3. Make caption attractive
4. Avoid jargons and use simple terms
5. Lead paragraph should be attractive

Awareness about principles for writing for rural readers is a must to be good writer. An analysis of awareness of farm magazines in Orissa was studied which yielded the following results. The writers before writing should have training for capacity building. Anybody can write but for better writing one has to acquire skill. It is our observation that many times the rural readers do not read farm magazines as it does not contain what he wants in his language and understanding.

Awareness and adoption of principles of writing news stories

1. Principles	Max. Obtainable score	Score value	Gap (%)
1. Purpose of writing	4.00	3.84	4.00
2. Knowledge about readers	4.00	3.10	22.50
3. Knowledge on Subject matter	4.00	2.85	28.75
4. Timely and immediate news	4.00	2.76	31.00
2. Principles	**Max. Obtainable score**	**Score Value**	**Gap (%)**
1. Simple and clear writing	4.00	2.45	38.75
2. Convincing	4.00	2.65	33.75
3. Absence of exaggeration	4.00	3.05	23.75
4. Use of personal words	4.00	2.80	30.00
3. Principles	**Max. Obtainable score**	**Score value**	**Gap (%)**
1. Right words and Short sentence	4.00	2.75	31.25
2. One sentence with one idea	4.00	2.50	37.50
3. Short paragraph and short Sentence	4.00	2.54	36.50
4. Principles	**Max. Obtainable score**	**Score Value**	**Gap (%)**
1. Specific points are keys to good news writing	4.00	2.30	42.50
2. Direct and meaningful Quotations increase interest.	4.00	2.00	50.00
3. Honesty in reporting and Writing is to be maintained.	4.00	3.40	15.00
5. Principles	**Max. Obtainable score**	**Score Value**	**Gap (%)**
1. Past tense and active voice are to be used.	4.00	2.95	6.25
2. Make caption attractive	4.00	2.80	30.00
3. Avoid jargons and use simple terms	4.00	3.05	23.75
4. Lead paragraph should be attractive	4.00	3.42	14.50

(Analysis of five farm magazine and 25 writers, Odisha)

Rules for writing News story

Certain rules make news story more effective and attractive. These are,

1. Short and brief
2. No repetition or unnecessary words
3. No negative words
4. No passive voice
5. Avoiding of ornamental words
6. Subject specific
7. Creation of interest to read
8. Good language and correct grammar
9. No mistake
10. Appropriate words and correct spelling
11. Simple words and style of writing
12. Technical words in simple language

6.8 Elements of news story

1. WHO

1. Who are readers?
2. Who is involved?
3. Who is affected?
4. Who supprt or oppose

2. WHEN

1. What is present status?
2. What the readers are doing
3. What can be done about it

3. WHERE

1. Where did it took place

4. WHAT

1. At what point story begins
2. Where it ends
3. Turning point in story
4. Next issue and time

5. WHY

1. Why people need it
2. Why the story is important
3. Why it happens

6. HOW

1. How the news was revealed
2. How the end has played out.
3. What can be done about it
4. How will add value to news

Procedure in writing the news story

Writer has to look into the following aspects and proceed to give final shape to news story.

1. Alertness about the happening around him
2. Know the format and standard of news paper where it will be published.
3. Keep ready the literature and clipping about the subject matter
4. Collect facts that are to go into news story
5. Write them in order of importance
6. Pick up most important and interesting points.
7. Write story in organized and logical manner
8. Develop rest of the story
9. Edit and rewrite
10. Give an impressive caption

Box No.2.18

Qualities of a farm journalist

1. Awareness
2. Alertness
3. Curiosity
4. Keen observation
5. Analytical bend of mind
6. A nose for news

13. Writing of feature story

A feature is a written composition of variable length intent to convey ideas and facts. It may be of variable length of small, medium or large.

It is difficult to differentiate feature story from news story. The difference is in emphasis. A feature story contains more details and description. Feature is amplification of idea while news story is of fictitious ideas. Editorials are not feature. Editorials are pinioned piece of writing representing views of editors and organization that publish news paper. Features are published in magazines not in news paper.

Features stories are stories of people, places and events. Local readers get more interested in feature stories. Good personalities, events of remembrance, community achievements are the major contents of feature stories.

Purpose of Feature story

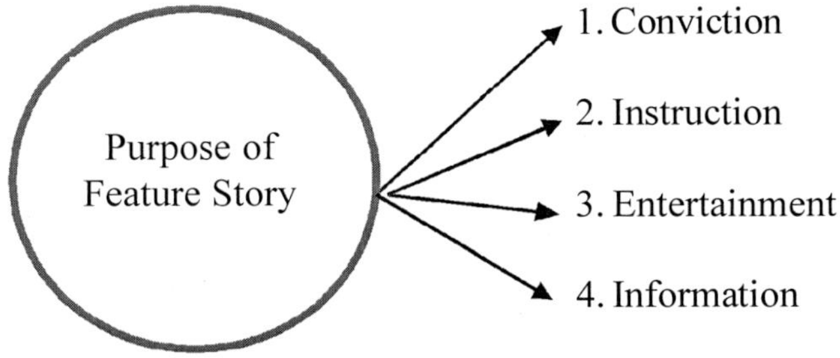

Characteristics of feature stories

Sometimes we confuse about news stories and feature stories. Feature stories are different than news stories.

1. After presentation of facts and ideas news stories stop while feature goes further to present details of information in depth.
2. It expresses details of back ground of the topic
3. It makes appeal to the mind of the readers and more personal to them
4. The writer has the freedom to write feature stories.

Preparation for writing features

Feature writing is a creative act. The writer has to get to prepare to create good features. The creativity has to be explored based on information. Preparation takes time and mind becomes heavy till writing starts. Experiences of good feature writers reveal that the following points are to be cared while preparation is made to write features.

1. New subject matter
2. Fitting to season of operation
3. Writing aims at wider circle of readers.
4. Enough information with specificity
5. Consideration of publication in which journal, magazine, and kind of readers.

Useful instructions for feature stories

When writer attempts to write feature story about a person, event, achievement or place, he has to be very much sensitive to the following steps to produce qualitative feature stories. The following steps have positive contribution for qualitative articles. The contribution of each step has been examined with farm feature writers (N=10)

Contribution of steps to quality articles as perceived by feature writers.

S.No.	Steps	% contribution
1.	Contact person, place, event personally	8.00
2.	Interview the person	0.00
3.	Use open ended question to collect information	5.00
4.	Maintain eye contact with interviewee	3.00
5.	Review answer after interview	11.00
6.	Identify main focus of the story	12.00
7.	Prepare outline of the story	9.00
8.	Write the story in creative mood	5.00
9.	Start with interesting fact	12.00
10.	Give description about person and achievement	9.00
11.	Present information in an interesting way	9.00
12.	Conclusion to include moral aspect	10.00
13.	Conclude to have impact on readers.	7.00
	Total	100.00

6.9 Procedures in writing of features

Every feature has three parts

1. Lead
2. Body
3. Conclusion

Each feature must have conclusion. News stories do not have it because readers do not require conclusion in news stories.

1. Lead

Lead in news stories and feature articles have same purpose. It attracts readers, creates interest so that reader read body and conclusion. Lead in feature articles is different from news stories. News stories have one kind of approach but features are lengthy in composition and require more efforts. Lead in feature article serves three functions.

i) Attract attention of reader

ii) Lead readers to body of the article

iii) Lead is to bridge initial part between lead to the body of articles.

The lead has three distinct sections in feature writing. These are teaser section, text section and Bridge.

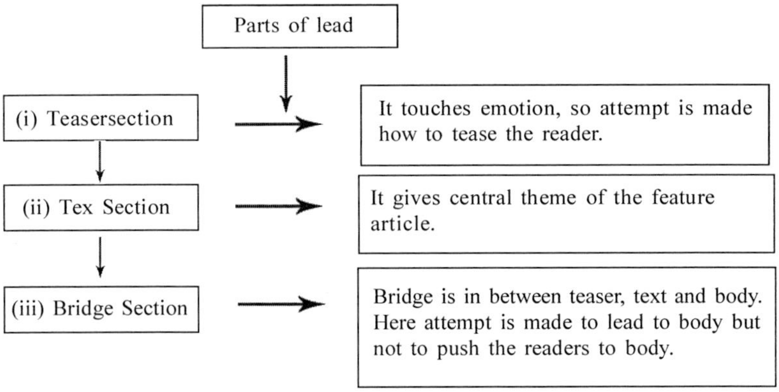

Types of Leads in Feature Article

The feature writer has great latitude in selecting lead. The choice is limitless. The lead may be of one of the followings.

1. News summery lead – This is similar to the lead in a news story. It contains five Ws - who, what, where, and why.
2. Short Sentence lead – This consists of a single striking sentence like, I was born with a silver spoon in my mouth.
3. Quotation lead –The sayings of a renowned person, poet or leader may be taken as lead, like, Necessity is the mother of Invention.
4. Question lead – Sometimes a question may provide a feature with an attractive lead like – Does life imitate art?
5. Contrast lead – Conflict and contrast many times provide a feature with lead which may bring forth the controversial nature of the feature. Like Economic situation looked quite rosy a years ago.
6. Picture lead – This gives voiced description of the setting of the feature or evokes a mood or feelings.
7. Humorous lead – A humorous lead sets the tone of a feature perfectly for the reader like, long experience has taught me that nobody goes to theatre unless he has bronchitis.
8. Anecdote lead – It is very popular. It can be fitted to any kind of article except process or utility features. It is very suitable for personality.
9. Striking statement lead – It arouse interest of reader by giving a mental shock so that he needs little persuasion to jump into the body. If not based on fact you may antagonize the readers.

10. Narrative lead – It is suitable for history, biography, personality known as very strong lead. The narrative lead does not lead to climax like once upon a time. Introduction to full story will come from lead.
11. Direct lead – Like readers are addressed as, You have to scarify for the nation.

2. Body of the feature

Body of the feature contains important materials in detail. Feature body is not different from other narrative writing. A feature should conform to the basic principles of good writing. For writing body you have to make arrangement at pre-writing stage. Think about idea, collect materials and keep in file.

1. Prepare – Prepare an outline. At pre-writing stage some exercise has to be made. Body should be tied to introduction or lead of the article.
2. Writing – Try to write easily, understandable accurate facts, correct language, interesting, smooth. First thought, logically leads to second thought, give appropriate paragraph, treatment to subject matter, accurate, complete coverage, add humour to writing, and lastly take out unnecessary things from the body.

   Rewriting – Rewriting is taken up to remove dullness.

Reasons of dullness

a) Use of too familiar contents, expression, like India is an Agricultural Country.
b) Verbosity – Big words, many words, adjectives
c) Use of words that are too general statements like small farmers are poor
d) Too abstract ideas – Give abstract ideas to save face. In order to give accurate information write not 79.9% but 80%.
e) Lack of dramatization – Write to sell ideas use salesmanship method by good thought and good language
f) Lack of rhythm – Continuity, smoothness in writing is essential, absence of this dullness appear in writing.

3. Conclusion

A news report does not need a conclusion. But a feature often though thought not always does. The conclusion may be a summing up of the feature or a climax as a short story or cutback or a flask back to the lead. n feature, conclusion and lead may be equally important in some cases. Writer keeps ending in mind while writing. We have to give careful thought, lingering ending is not desirable.

In feature article (a) promise what to do (b) tell or (c) say what you have said. At the end writer may ask to himself.

i) What is the purpose of writing?

ii) For whom is the writing i.e. nature of readers

iii) What has been achieved by this writing?

iv) Did I talk to the same audience through out

These questions make writer sensible about his article

Type of ending

Ending points need assurance from readers to act on the message. It should be short, concise and pin pointing.

1. Pleasant ending – Evoke laugh in the face of the reader.
2. Summary ending – Tell audience what has been said in article and present in summary form.
3. Action ending – Ask readers to act on idea.
4. Illustrating ending – Classical quotation, analogy or a story to keep everlasting.
5. Flash back ending – Take back reader to beginning where you started. Like do you still insist to use old methods?

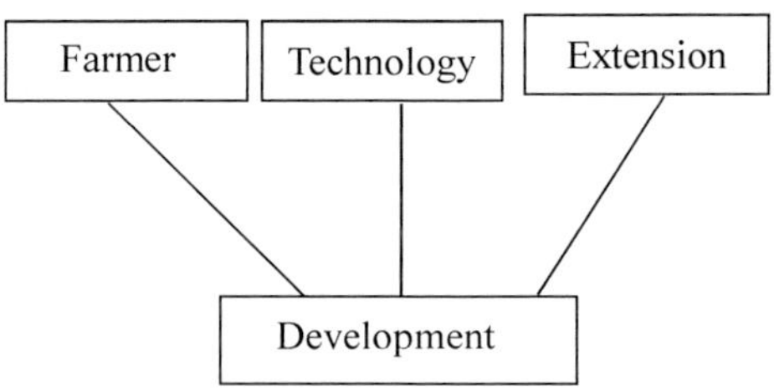

Collection of Materials for writing

Writing material refers to the materials that provide the surfaces on which humans use writing instruments to inscribe writings. The same materials can also be used for symbolic or representational drawings. Building material on which writings or drawings are produced is not included

Sourcing and Collecting Materials

You might be looking for-

- **Ideas and opinions** – expert opinion, opinions of pressure groups, public opinion, opinion of companies involved in trials, opinion of governments and other organisations, parents' concerns

- **Research results** – medical experiments, scientific information
- **History** – where the debate began and why, specific cases which make the vaccine questionable

Once you have a clear idea of what you need to know about your topic to deal with the assignment posed, you will be able to look more closely at the individual resources available to you, such as database, to see what information they contain. You will need to weigh up the relevance of the information you find, and develop a critical awareness of the positions represented in what you read – in some cases, authors may be explicitly expressing a particular viewpoint but in others there may be hidden bias, which can be misleading.

Don't forget that one of the best ways to source relevant material for your essay is to 'snowball' your reading: i.e. to use the footnotes and bibliographies of the books you already have to extend your reading list on a subject. Your reading lists will already include many of the most important writers; by checking their bibliographies and works cited in those articles, you will have access to the most up-to-date writing on the topic.

More notes on researching material

Your literature review

At some point in your research activities you will have to produce a comprehensive and critical summary of the current and past research in your subject area. This summary is often called a literature review but other names include: state-of-the-art-review, topic review and subject review.

In order to produce a good literature review you will need to be regularly identifying and reviewing relevant material (more on this later). Your literature review will only be as good as the material you find and it is essential to understand how information in your field is published and how to search for it. You may find that you have to carry out a literature search at several points in the research process.

At the beginning you may want to do a search to

- Improve your knowledge of the subject area
- Get ideas about how to conduct research in your area
- Identify gaps in the current body of knowledge
- Identify trends and predict future developments
- Identify keywords/terms and phrases
- Identify key people and organizations.

In the middle of the research process you may wish to review the literature to

- Review your own progress or re-evaluate your position
- Check for new research findings that may impact on your research
- Check for relevant literature in related fields
- Use keywords you hadn't thought of before.

When writing up your research you may use the review to

- Check for new research findings that may impact on your research
- Introduce your topic
- Place your research in context
- Support your findings or research methods
- Demonstrate understanding of your subject area.

Precisely what constitutes a literature review will vary with subject as well as purpose. You will need to check with your supervisor or review board. There are many guides available that explain how to conduct literature searches and literature reviews.

The shape of the literature

To be an effective researcher requires a good knowledge of the information resources in your subject area. This 'subject knowledge' encompasses not only the ability to understand and critically evaluate relevant information, but also an awareness of and an ability to utilise the full range of information sources in your area. A blanket term used to describe all of the relevant, inter-related information sources in one subject area is 'the shape of the literature'.

What is the shape of *my* literature?

The shape of the literature varies between subject areas. This is because information resources differ between subject areas, with some subjects having unique resources; for example maps in cartography. Also, due to their broad subject coverage, some information resources are common to many subject areas; for example ISI Web of Knowledge. The relative importance of these resources, however, may be different.

Another aspect of the shape of the literature that differs between subjects is the use of the terms primary and secondary literature. These terms are used differently in different disciplines. In some scientific disciplines, journal articles are referred to as primary sources of literature with books as a secondary source. In some social sciences this distinction is reversed, with monographs (predominantly books) referred to as the primary literature and journal articles as the secondary source.

'Grey literature' is a term common to all subjects and means material that is not formally 'published', such as an institutional report. Grey literature can be difficult to trace.

As there is no agreement across disciplines on how to define the terms primary, secondary and grey literature, we suggest you find out what these terms mean in your subject area.

Resources useful for your research

A good literature review contains references to material from a broad range of resources. This is important even if your literature review covers a very narrow subject area.

The resources table lists 15 resources. You may find it useful to check through the entries and see if there are any resources that you have not searched yet. The column on the far right suggests ways to trace each resource. You can print out the table and keep it as an aide-memoire.

7

Presentation Techniques

"The ability to speak effectively is an acquirement rather than a gift"

– ***Willim Jennings Bryan***

Presentation takes place all the time in organization. We are required to make presentation in meeting, seminar, conference etc. The presenter should know certain techniques to make his presentation effective. In transfer of technology the presenter is expected to make his message clear and for that he should be well prepared.

7.1 A good presentation attracts the attention

A good presentation attracts the attention of the audience and they expect the message would meet their information needs. A person may be required to make presentation other than his core specialization. They will be under pressure to make a memorable presentation. Thecompetencies of the presenter will be tested in both verbal and non-verbal communication skill, knowledge of making slide presentation, ability to meet interpersonal skill while handling questions and objections on different opinions and finally a word of thanks. Effective presentation skill reflects the personality of the presenter. If well presented it will enhance the image of the presenter. Good presentation speaks about the confidence level, knowledge level, logical thinking, and range of ideas and practical value of the message.

7.2 Misconception about presentation

The speakers and presenters face problems. To hide the deficiencies people give different reasons. On practice many have achieved name and fame of being good presenters. Some of the misconceptions are,

1. Good speakers are born and not made

People speak smartly and fluently. It is not gift nor inherited but learned and practiced. One has to work hard to become a good speaker

2. Presentation is to practice, practice and more practice

The practical experience of many reveals that before giving presentation one has to practice many times to achieve competency. A person who is never nervous has to practice many times as the practice makes a man perfect. This is true for anybody at any time.

3. New Faces of the audience

Some speakers are scared looking at good gathering with new faces. They feel nervous. But the failure is the stepping stone to succed.If one knows the matter well he will easily face the new daces with good presentation

4. Deficiency in Language especially English

Many speakers talk of language problem especially English. One has to remember that presentations are a combination of matter and manner. When one knows matter well the words come automatically to make expression better.

5. Enjoyable presentation

The aim should be to make presentation enjoyable. Perfection lies there only to see the audience enjoy the presentation. Speaking to small or large audience demand,

i) Handle audience well.

ii) Know the subject well rather perfectly

iii) Sharpen skill of speaking

7.3 Getting ready for presentation

For making a successful presentation one simple thing is to be remembered that gathering of more information is not enough. The objective should be to make point or concept clear so as to make them comprehensible to the audience. It does not mean to memorise whole topic but aware of the content.

There are three important steps to get ready for presentation

1. **Developing a presentation:** What is topic and what is the purpose

   The topic and purpose of presentation should be clearly understood. What the presentation aims at should be perfectly decided before preparing the slides for presentation. The purpose of presentation like to make aware or to be in action should be in the mind of the presenter.

2. **Knowledge about the audience:** Knowing audience

   Who are the audience, who will be listening, and how large in size, details of composition of audience, their status, in term of technical back ground are the important information a presenter should know. Such information will strengthen the presenter to present his message.

3. **Presentation:** How to deliver the message and expectation of audience

Communication is message perceived not message sent. The entire focus of the presentation on the content and delivery that must be directed towards the audience. The audience must understand what is said so that they can participate in listening process and ask question. Therefore a good presentation has to be well conceptualized broke down to separate parts and researched extensively. Some important questions are to be answered at this stage.

i) Appealing of topic to audience
ii) Relating topic to practical life
iii) Holding the attention of the audience
iv) How many writings, pictures, graphs would be required for presentation
v) Expectation of audience
vi) How to start and close the presentation.

7.3 Style and structure of presentation

According to Micki Holliday the presentation style is of three types

i) Cool zone
ii) Hot zone
iii) Dull zone

i) Cool Zone

In this case the presenter keeps the psychology of the audience in mind and presents matter from their view point. The presenter with clear persuasive skill presents the matter. The presentation is structured one, facts are presented in an orderly manner and delivery is under control. The pitch, volume, and tone all are under control. The thoughtful manner of presentation makes audience friendly to the subject matter.

ii) Hot zone

In this case loud voice, rhetorical style, dramatic body movement and voice inflections describe such a speaker belonging to hot zone. Because they are driven by passions their pitch keeps going ups and downs, the loudness of voice matching pitch level supported by body movement daring eyes and shifting postures. Some audience enjoy such presentation and some dislike.

3. Dull zone

In this case presentation is boring. They lack of pitch variation, unpromising body language and incompatibility with the audience. Nervous body language tremors in the voice, poor eye contact rushing off with the matter horridly make the speaker dull one.

7.4 Tips for presentation

Once we have visualized that our presentation is going to be successful because we have researched and practiced matter well. The presenter has to stand be for audience confidently to give presentation. There are few tips to make good presentation.

1. Introduction
2. Body language
3. Capturing attention of the audience
4. Closing up
5. Handling questions.
6. Qualities of a skilful presenter

1. Introduction

Opening with words of thank to chairperson and audience. The presenter should know that he stands before audience he is scanned by them. Better come straight to topic because audience do not like to waste time.

2. Body Language

i) Stand straight, hold head high, keep shoulders straight not dropping.
ii) Standing firmly enhances stature and gives tremendous self confidence
iii) Helps hands well. An open palm gesture integrates well with an open body language.
iv) Common errors are to be avoided are putting face down, awkward posture, stiff body, low or fast voice.

3. Capturing attention of the audience

All presentation has a broad frame work. The main objectives are to inform, persuade, inspire and convince. When matter is delivered using illustrations, facts, and figures continuously move towards predetermined conclusions.

i) Begin confidently by speaking slowly and less loudly keeping voice under control.

ii) Do not speak in a demanding manner

iii) Deliver with confidence and humility

iv) Visual aids, audience and speaking tone to be in one line

v) Focusing on subject with smiling face

vi) Follow introduction, body, and conclusion as format of talk.

vii) Emphasize benefits of the audience and need to know.

4. Closing up

The conclusion is an important part of the presentation because it is the part of audience that they will carry back with them and remember the message. A quick recap of the points can be reviewed. At the end do not forget to thank the audience for listening.

5. Handling questions

An insightful and intelligent presenter always anticipates questions from the audience. Often there may be hostile or resistant listeners and likely out questions. There is need to handle the m carefully.

i) Encourage audience to ask question

ii) Listen to the question very well

ii) Compliant the person asking question

iv) Those who ask question for sake of asking question to be handled carefully.

v) Do not let few people to dominate question session.

Be careful about important points for good presentation

1.	Content	Poorly researched matter
2.	Speech	Talking rapidly, lack of clarity, wrong pronunciation
3.	Voice	High pitch, talking down at audience, mumbling tone
4.	Face	Unsmiling poor, eye contact
5.	Gesture	Hand in pocket, arm crossed
6.	Language	Poor grammar, long sentence
7.	Style	Lack of confidence, indirect communication beating about bush, poor content, no proper introduction

6. Qualities of a skilful presenter

1.	Self control	No feeling of nervous
2.	Poise	Good command on body language
3.	Awareness	Of people, time, and place. Full knowledge of guidance, time and venue
4.	Tact	Ability to blend with audience and matter
5.	Decisiveness	Very clear about matter
6.	Persuasiveness	Ability to make audience to see important points
7.	Enthusiasm	Never loose sight of objective of presentation
8.	Honesty	Not faking knowledge or information
9.	Flexibility	Not to be rigid if opinion differs

References

Adler, B. Ronald and J.M. Elmhorst (1966). Communicating at Work. McGraw Hill Companies, Inc.Toronto.

Alessandra, Tony, and Phil Hunsaker (1993). Communicating at Work A fireside Book. Singapore.

Berlo, D.K. (1960). A process of Communication. Holt Rinechart and Wingtone Inc. New York.

Boober, Dianna (2003). Speak with Confidence. Powerful Presentation That informs, inspires and Persuade. McGrew Hill Toronto.

Bryson, Lyman (1936). Communication of ideas. Harper, New York.

Dahama, O.P. and Bhatnagar (2003). Education and Communication for Development. Mohan Primlani for Oxford and IBH Publishing Co. Pvt. Ltd. New Delhi.

Fast Julius (1971). Body Talk: The Skills of Positive Image Excel Book, New Delhi.

Harvard Business (1999). Review on Effective communication Harvard Business School Press.

Kelsy and Hearne, G.C. (1963). Co-operative Extension Work, Comestock Publishing Associate, New York.

Leagans, J.P. (1961). Communication Process in Rural Development. Cornell University Ithaca, New York.

Lewis, Hedwig (1998). Body Language: A guide for Professionals. Response Books. New Delhi.

Mack, Angela (1970). The language of business. The English Book Store. New Delhi.

Maunder, J.L. (1955). Agriculture Extension. A reference Manual, FAO. Rome.

Miculka, Jean (1999). Speaking for Success. South-Western Educational Publishing, Washington.

Pareek, U. and Singh, Y.P. (1968). Socio-Economic Characteristics of Key Communicators. Sociological Bulletin X.VI

Ray, G.L. (2001). Extension Communication and Management, Naya Prokash 2006, Bidhan Sarani Calcutta.

Roger, E.M. and Shoemaker, F.P. (1971). Communication of Innovations. The Free Press, New York.

Satapathy, C. and Das, R.N. (2000). Communication and Farm Journalism. Golden Graphics Publication, Bhubaneswar.

Sen, L. (2004). Communication Skill Prentice Hall India, New Delhi.

Steinberg, C.S. (1958). The Mass Communication. New York, Happer and Bros.

Timm. T. Paul (1986). Managerial Communication: A Finger onh the Pulse. Prentice Hall. Inc. New Jersey.